Georgia

A Captivating Guide to the History of the Peach State and the Cherokees

© Copyright 2023 - All rights reserved.

The content contained within this book may not be reproduced, duplicated, or transmitted without direct written permission from the author or the publisher.

Under no circumstances will any blame or legal responsibility be held against the publisher, or author, for any damages, reparation, or monetary loss due to the information contained within this book, either directly or indirectly.

Legal Notice:

This book is copyright protected. It is only for personal use. You cannot amend, distribute, sell, use, quote, or paraphrase any part, or the content within this book, without the consent of the author or publisher.

Disclaimer Notice:

Please note the information contained within this document is for educational and entertainment purposes only. All effort has been executed to present accurate, up-to-date, reliable, and complete information. No warranties of any kind are declared or implied. Readers acknowledge that the author is not engaging in the rendering of legal, financial, medical, or professional advice. The content within this book has been derived from various sources. Please consult a licensed professional before attempting any techniques outlined in this book.

By reading this document, the reader agrees that under no circumstances is the author responsible for any losses, direct or indirect, that are incurred as a result of the use of the information contained within this document, including, but not limited to, errors, omissions, or inaccuracies.

Free Bonus from Captivating History (Available for a Limited time)

Hi History Lovers!

Now you have a chance to join our exclusive history list so you can get your first history ebook for free as well as discounts and a potential to get more history books for free! Simply visit the link below to join.

Captivatinghistory.com/ebook

Also, make sure to follow us on Facebook, Twitter and Youtube by searching for Captivating History.

Table of Contents

PART 1: HISTORY OF GEORGIA 1
    INTRODUCTION 2
    CHAPTER 1 – PRE-EXPLORATION GEORGIA 4
    CHAPTER 2 – BRITISH COLONIZATION 13
    CHAPTER 3 – GEORGIA AND THE REVOLUTIONARY WAR 22
    CHAPTER 4 – SLAVERY IN GEORGIA 31
    CHAPTER 5 – ANTEBELLUM GEORGIA 37
    CHAPTER 6 – CIVIL WAR AND RECONSTRUCTION 47
    CHAPTER 7 – DEMOCRATIC GEORGIA AND WORLD WAR II 60
    CHAPTER 8 – CIVIL RIGHTS ERA 67
    CHAPTER 9 – CARTER YEARS 74
    CHAPTER 10 – MODERN GEORGIA 80
    CONCLUSION 82
PART 2: THE CHEROKEES 84
    INTRODUCTION 85
    CHAPTER 1 – ANI′-YÛÑ′ WIYĂ′ 88
    CHAPTER 2 – EARLY CONFLICTS WITH THE EUROPEAN SETTLERS 94
    CHAPTER 3 – A TIME OF TREATIES AND COMPROMISES 99
    CHAPTER 4 – THE ASSIMILATION OF THE CHEROKEE 104
    CHAPTER 5 – THE BEGINNINGS OF THE GREAT REMOVAL 109
    CHAPTER 6 – THE TRAIL OF TEARS 116

CHAPTER 7 - AN EXAMINATION OF THE TRAIL OF TEARS FROM A MODERN VIEWPOINT 122
CHAPTER 8 - UNSTABLE TIMES IN OKLAHOMA 128
CHAPTER 9 - A BRIEF HISTORY OF RESIDENTIAL SCHOOLS 141
CHAPTER 10 - THE CHEROKEE IN THE 20TH AND 21ST CENTURIES 150
CONCLUSION 156
HERE'S ANOTHER BOOK BY CAPTIVATING HISTORY THAT YOU MIGHT LIKE 159
FREE BONUS FROM CAPTIVATING HISTORY (AVAILABLE FOR A LIMITED TIME) 160
ENDNOTES 161

Part 1: History of Georgia

A Captivating Guide to the People and Events That Shaped the History of the Peach State of the United States of America

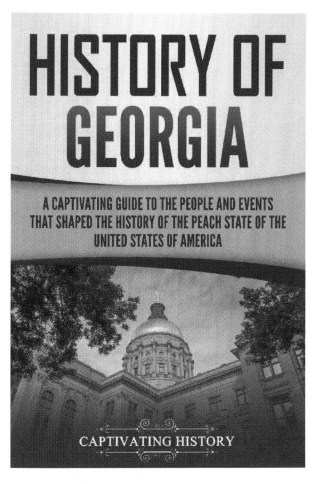

Introduction

If we're being honest, anyone who has sat through a middle school US history class can tell you most of the highlights of what happened in the early days of that fledgling country. European explorers arrived. They took land and spread disease, wiping out entire people groups. Then, the British came and held the first Thanksgiving. The colonies were established, and there was a big revolution. America was born. And then, the country split over politics and slavery but came back together in a messy kind of reconciliation before continuing to suppress the rights of an entire people group (again).

Accurate or not, that is typically the list.

When we move further through United States history, we see that most states are an amalgam of the same dates and events. A colony gets settled by a group of (typically) persecuted people, fight against the British, gain independence, become a state, form a government, write a state constitution, make decisions about slavery, take sides in the Civil War and the ongoing slave debate, and then enter our current modern era after the civil rights movement of the 1950s and 1960s.

Because of these easily divisible sections of time, most states are assumed to think, legislate, and live a certain way. Some of them are changed by history, others are hardened by it, and some see very little change. That assumption is a hard one to break, especially when it just seems like the pitter-patter of history goes on and on and on and—well, you get it.

But what if I told you one of the largest states in the Southeast doesn't fit that mold? Or, at the very least, has broken it wide open?

What if I told you that before US history was writing its story, Georgia was writing one of its own? That at every beat of the American story, Georgia was going against the grain?

Georgia's history is more than just peaches. It's a story of prisoners, preachers, peanuts, and presidents who rose above the status quo to help transform more than just their nation but also the entire world. Join me as we walk through some of the victories and disappointments, along with some honest evaluations, that shaped Georgia as we (may not) know it.

Chapter 1 – Pre-Exploration Georgia

Long before the first prisoners were ever shipped to the thirteenth American colony, Georgia was home to thousands of years' worth of Native American history. Many artifacts and tribal markings still remain all across Georgia, waiting patiently to be discovered and preserved.

The Paleoindian (pronounced: Pal-e-o-indian) period was a three- to six-thousand-year-long period in which the Clovis people groups entered and lived nomadically throughout Georgia.[1] Some details still remain unclear about the Paleoindian groups like the Clovis. What we do know, however, is that they moved throughout the land in groups of twenty-five to fifty, and when they would temporarily settle, it was in areas where they could find the resources necessary to create their tell-tale arrowheads: lance-shaped with small cut-outs near the bottom. These settlements would have been near quarries. Historians can conclude they used small boats and walked on land to get from resource to resource.

One unclear fact remains about the Clovis: what did they eat? Were their arrows for large game hunting or defense? Those answers may be found by looking at the world the Clovis lived in. Due to global weather conditions at the time, the world looked incredibly different. The oceans

---

[1] There is some debate as to the length of this period; in order to honor that discretion, we have thought it best to give the full range of its potential length.

and gulfs around that part of modern America were much further removed from land than they are today, larger creatures were beginning to go extinct, and pine forests covered much of modern Georgia—a far cry from the hardwoods seen in small pockets across the state now. All of this may indicate that the Clovis mostly had a vegetarian diet with small game added when the occasion allowed.

Like with most cultures, as time progressed, the Clovis and other Paleoindian groups began to lose their nomadic ways and settled down to make villages. Because of these villages, historians have uncovered a variety of artifacts. The Paleoindians were able to leave behind a variety of icons and tribal markers.

There are more than just small, temporary icons, though.

The 102-foot-tall Rock Eagle in Eatonton (Putnam County) is a permanent part of Georgia's landscape. The pseudo-cobblestone eagle is laid out as an effigy, although we do not know who it is in honor of. Other Paleoindian markers across the state include stone walls and stone mounds, both of which have confounded archaeologists as to their purpose. It is inconclusive if the stone mounds, some of which are three feet tall, were used as grave markers or were simply moved and stacked as some sort of cultural habit.

While the stone mounds may puzzle archaeologists, the purpose of the remaining stone walls is clear: defense.

As the land thawed and the climate regulated itself, the water-rich and mild land of what is now Georgia became a hub of native settlements. Over time, these small settlements of twenty-five to fifty began to grow as families multiplied and resources became more readily available through early forms of farming. Out of necessity, chiefdoms were established to give order to the new and growing societies.

As you can imagine, as several settlements began to grow into villages (each with its own identity), there was a need to compete for resources with other groups. The competition got worse as more and more tribes moved into the resource-rich land of modern Georgia.

The infighting couldn't last for too long, though, as a mutual enemy was on its way: European explorers.

With the arrival of the European explorers, the tribal culture in 16th-century Georgia evolved rapidly, not because the tribes wanted to but because they had to in order to survive, as you will see in the next section.

These once varied and thriving tribes were ravaged by disease and fighting, and they eventually merged to form the Creek and Cherokee societies. The Creeks dominated the south and southeast of Georgia, while the Cherokee held land in the north along the Blue Ridge Mountains.

The Creek Nation

According to Claudio Saunt, a professor of early American history, "The history of early Georgia is largely the history of the Creek Indians."[2]

As we said before, a lot changed for the native populations in Georgia immediately before European explorers arrived. The effects of exploration, especially the spread of disease, did great harm to the newly settled native villages, most especially near the Ocmulgee and Chattahoochee Rivers. You have to remember that water travel was faster for natives than walking on foot. The Native Americans who settled along these major waterways were very susceptible to incursion by diseased explorers.

It was not until the late 17th century that most of the affected populations began to recover.

And so, the Creeks were born.

While it was not the native peoples' intention to become one nation, it happened nonetheless. The Creek Nation began as a cooperative, loose alliance of the disease-weakened tribes west of the Ocmulgee River in Georgia and east of the rivers Coosa and Tallapoosa located in Alabama. Achieving peaceable relations was more important to these pockets of natives than their differences (they spoke at least three but probably more languages, including Muskogee, Alabama, and Hitchiti). Each native group seemed intent on keeping its tribal identity until it began to trade with colonists in South Carolina. These colonists began calling the cooperative tribes "Creeks" to indicate they were the "Indians living on Ochese Creek."[3] As time went on, all the Native Americans in the area were called Creeks by the traders they worked with.

The trade the Creeks did with these South Carolinians paved the way for relations with James Oglethorpe and company when they arrived in Georgia; we'll talk about these folks in just a bit. At the time, the Creeks outnumbered these new white colonists and the enslaved people from

---

[2] Saunt, Claudio. "Creek Indians." New Georgia Encyclopedia, last modified Aug 25, 2020.

[3] Saunt, Claudio. "Creek Indians."

Africa who came with them. The Creeks also occupied more land, although that would later change.

By 1715, the trade for deerskins was well established, replacing the slave trade of other native peoples from Florida. The main commodities provided to the Creeks were European textiles, kettles, guns, and rum. The Port of Savannah, built in 1744, became central to the Creek deerskin trade: by the late 1750s, it is estimated that up to sixty thousand deerskins were shipped through Savannah.

Relations between the colonists and Creeks thrived for many years. Some colonists even settled in Creek villages, married Creek women, and had children who might even grow up to be tribal leaders. The relationships between the traders and Creeks worked to encourage the Creeks to begin plantations of their own, which had limited success. African slaves, even escaped slaves from farther up the coast, settled on Creek lands. As a result, the Creeks learned of the horrors of slavery and began to disavow the practice.

Unfortunately, the good relationship between the Creeks and the colonists would not last forever.

From 1790 to 1805, several treaties were forced onto the Creeks by the state of Georgia that ceded Creek lands east of the Ocmulgee River to the state. The first of these, the Treaty of New York, established an official leader for the Creek Nation, which previously had a scrappy, decentralized system for politics. Another initiative by the United States intended to turn many of the Creeks into farmers or ranchers. This initiative was embraced by some but not all, and it led to a civil war within the Creek Nation that only ended due to US involvement. The US forces were led by General Andrew Jackson. In 1814, eight hundred Creeks were killed by the US military before the Red Stick War came to an end. With the signing of the treaty, twenty-two million acres of Creek land were ceded to the United States, including a lot of territory in southern Georgia.

By 1836, after several more conflicts, failed treaties, and bribed native leaders, the Creek Nation was forcibly rounded up by the United States military and the Georgia and Alabama militias. The Creeks were sent off to what would become the Oklahoma Territory along the Trail of Tears. This, for the most part, was the end of the Creeks' involvement in Georgia's history.

The Cherokee Nation

The Cherokee have a few distinct differences from the Creek Nation. These differences are not like saying, "A truck is different from a car because a truck has a cargo bed and a car does not." Rather, the things that set the Cherokee apart made them *distinctly* Cherokee in a way no other native at the time could claim.

To begin with, the Cherokee were different from the Creeks in that the Cherokee were one people. They were not a mixed bag of post-exploration survivors who banded together. The Cherokee had been and always would be a distinct people in their own right.

One Cherokee distinction was their language. The Cherokee spoke an Iroquoian language that was different from their neighbors who favored a Muskogean, Algonquian, or Siouan language base.[4]

The Cherokee also had a common homeland in the southern Appalachian Mountains, which was called Blue Ridge' in its Georgian portion. With this shared geographical heritage also came kinship networks that bound them together. These networks helped to define who was and who was not a member of the Cherokee Nation.

Even with all of these unique and unifying characteristics, the Cherokee were not perfect. See what Boulware has to say about tribal unity:

> "Though a shared cultural heritage and political connections also conjoined the Cherokees into a recognizable ethnic group, they were far from a united people. Social, political, and religious activity centered on the local village. They organized themselves into the divisions known during the Historic Period: the Overhill Towns, the Middle Towns, the Out Towns, the Valley Towns, and the Lower Towns. The latter two made up the Cherokee inhabitants of Georgia.
>
> Regionalism further generated divisions ... These varying locations and identities influenced the ways in which Cherokees interacted with outsiders."[5]

As we continue, it will be clear how the interaction with and influence of outsiders has a rather important impact on the health and values of the Cherokee moving forward in history.

---

[4] Boulware, Tyler. "Cherokee Indians." New Georgia Encyclopedia, last modified Aug 24, 2020.

[5] Boulware, Tyler. "Cherokee Indians."

The Cherokee Nation had a similar history to all of the native groups in the Southeast. They were nomadic for most of history, built mounds across their territories, faced disease and collapsing chiefdoms with the arrival of Europeans, and regrouped after that period. Where their history in the Southeast diverts is how they were able to maintain relations with the British traders in the Carolina territory (which later became territories).

The Cherokee worked to edge out rival tribes to secure sole trading rights with the British. Their culture was impacted by trade; they were "early adopters" (to use modern technology lingo). They traded primarily out of Augusta, Georgia, and Charleston, South Carolina. Like the Creeks, traders often lived in Cherokee settlements. By adopting technology so quickly, the Cherokee (perhaps unintentionally) tipped the scales of power in the region. Because they had such a chokehold on the region's native-to-British trade, many other settlers and indigenous groups became jealous. This led to a series of conflicts for the Cherokee.

The first large conflict later became known as the Yamasee War (1715-1717). Right after the Carolinas were split and the Cherokees were beginning to have exclusive trading rights, the Yamasee warred against the Carolinians with their allied groups. Their claim for war was British trade abuses and land encroachment on tribal territory. Because the Cherokee were tied to this trade, they intervened. However, they were not on the side of the Yamasee; they assisted the British, solidifying their grasp over the "new" Carolina territories.

Shortly after, the Cherokee killed a delegation of Creeks who were advocating against the establishment of the Carolina territories. While this might have galvanized the British-Cherokee relationship, it lit the spark for a forty-year war between the Cherokees and Creeks. As a result, the Creeks kept mostly to Georgia but would sometimes venture into French Louisiana as time progressed.

For the Cherokee, this was when friendly relations with the British peaked and then slowly began to decline. Moving forward, the Cherokee would never have relationships with the colonists (and, later, Americans) that were so equitable.

After assisting the British in the French and Indian War (1754-1763), which was part of the larger Seven Years' War, the Cherokee-British relationship went downhill. The Cherokee did not feel as though their one thousand warriors (a full third of their fighting force) were compensated enough for their efforts to rout the French. As a result of the deteriorating relations, the Cherokee moved into other parts of North America and shamelessly raided several Virginia backcountry settlements. As you might believe, these raids were not well received, and a series of conflicts and murders took place between the settlers and the Cherokees.

These raids led to open conflict, later named the Anglo-Cherokee War (1759-1761). This war ended with several Cherokee villages across Georgia and the Carolinas being torched and razed by the British military and colonists. The displaced Cherokee were made all the more susceptible to the spread of smallpox, suffering large population loss and waiting years for their villages to be even partially restored.

By the time the American Revolution came around, the Cherokee were not interested in assisting the land-hungry colonists who had harmed their people a decade earlier. Instead, they backed the British, even though most of the Cherokees wanted to remain neutral. They continued raiding backcountry settlements and went as far as to wage open warfare with the southern colonies during the war, including Georgia.

The hostilities did not end, however.

> "[M]any villagers sought peace with the Americans ... a large contingent of warriors continued to fight and relocated their towns to north Georgia ... They continued to war against the United States for more than a decade after the Treaty of Paris (1783) ended the Revolution. Only after repeated invasions of their homeland did the Chickamauga Cherokees finally agree to end hostilities."[6]

One of the tragedies of Cherokee history is that when it is foiled against the Creeks, you cannot ask but wonder what went wrong. Why did it have to be this way?

Like many other people, nations, and groups across all of history, the Cherokee ended up backing the wrong horse—in their case, the British. While the opportunity for trade with colonists existed, they instead chose to do so with the British. When given the chance to support their neighboring indigenous peoples against the British, they chose to prioritize trade and new technologies. And as the American Revolution began around them, they again chose to partner with the British in the hopes of

---

[6] Boulware, Tyler. "Cherokee Indians."

preserving their lands.

Geography and culture contributed to this result as well. Historians often agree that the Middle Colonies had some of the worst native relations after the first colonial settlements were established in the early 1600s. The Cherokee, who had settled all throughout the Appalachian area, were naturally more likely to follow this pattern as opposed to, say, the Creeks in the Deep South, whose relations deteriorated many years after the Revolutionary War.

Regardless, though, the final fate of the Cherokee is the same as their indigenous neighbors: the Trail of Tears. From the end of the American Revolution to 1820, a series of treaties with the American government began to erode Cherokee land control. In the 1820s and 1830s, Georgia began a campaign to aggressively remove the Cherokee people from the land rather than just letting time and treaties take it away. The legislature passed several articles that gave more control of those lands to the state, and the lands were later given to white settlers in a lottery.

With the Indian Removal Act of 1830 and a failed period of negotiations, the Cherokee were forcibly removed from their territory in Georgia and headed for modern-day Oklahoma.

Spanish Exploration in Brief

The arrival of the Spanish to the Americas looked different in Georgia than in most other areas. This will be a trend of early Georgian history that cannot be repeated enough: things were just different in Georgia!

In most Spanish colonies, Spain created forts and largely forced native populations to attend missionary classes. Interestingly, there was a short-lived six-week-long expedition across Georgia by Lúcas Vázquez de Ayllón in 1526. While missionaries often accompanied explorations, there was no long-term investment in the Georgia territory. A variety of missions took place from 1568 to 1684, but none took root, and the Spanish kept their focus on the Gulf Coast and Florida. However, even without taking a permanent hold, the missions throughout the Georgia territory helped to introduce and assimilate some native groups to Spanish and (eventually) English colonization.

While the Spanish failed to set up any permanent settlements in Georgia, the English would eventually add their final colony there after years of trade. Had the Spanish been able to establish themselves in

Georgia, we can be assured that the United States as we know it today would be a vastly different country.

Chapter 2 – British Colonization

Imagine for a moment that a new apartment building has gone up downtown. You do not know too much about it, but what you've heard has made you wonder what things will be like for those who live there.

Then, one night on the news, you hear, "This just in. The city council has announced its plans for the new thirteen-story apartment downtown! The mayor, on behalf of the council, has stated that each floor of the apartment will house people of all different backgrounds and goals." As you continue listening to this strange update, the news anchor begins announcing a few of those groups. "Six floors will be dedicated to different religious sects. Businessmen and landowners will operate out of a few floors. The friend of the mayor is being given full control of an entire floor (he'll decide who moves in later!)."

Just when you thought it couldn't get any stranger, you hear who will be living on the thirteenth floor. "And, finally, the council has come together to announce that the top floor will be used to house white-collar criminals.

Now, we can all acknowledge how ridiculous an idea that seems. No one would ever expect that such a strangely varied apartment building would ever exist, and they're probably right! Regardless, though, this situation is similar to how America looked in the early days of colonization. Massachusetts, Connecticut, Pennsylvania, Maryland, Rhode Island, and Virginia (among other reasons) were all founded on some religious pretense.

- **Massachusetts** was founded due to persecution in England by the Church of England. Two separate groups began settling Massachusetts: the Separatists (who we often call the Pilgrims) and the Puritans (who came from England after traveling there from northern Europe), a portion of whom later split off from its founding group and established **Connecticut**.
- **Pennsylvania** was a haven for Quaker Christians who followed William Penn, the disgraced son of Sir William Penn, admiral and politician. (William Penn the younger was disgraced because of his beliefs: he was a pacifist. Believe it or not, his highly honored father was none too pleased by his son's religious belief that fighting was ungodly.)
- **Maryland** was the Catholics' home in America due to persecution by the Church of England. It was aptly named after the Catholic queen, Henrietta Maria, wife of Charles I.
- **Rhode Island** was established by Roger Williams due to persecution he faced by churches in the New World. His close ties to the Native American population and desire to convert them made him a pariah among church leaders. He established Rhode Island as the first colony to uphold religious liberty. No religious group was excluded from practicing there.
- **Virginia** was both a cash crop venture by England and a foothold for the Church of England in the Americas, though the Church of England would struggle for decades to keep its footing in the Colony of Virginia, and it would only get worse after statehood.

New Hampshire, New York, Delaware, New Jersey, and both Carolinas were all established for trade and/or farming. The dominant trade in the early years was beaver fur with the native tribes and French settlers in modern-day Canada. The primary cash crops of the colonies were tobacco and indigo, but it would later become cotton since growing conditions were favorable for it.

Then, at the bottom of the coastline, there was Georgia. The final colony has a strange and often misunderstood founding as a colony.

The rumor mill of history has often, at best, misrepresented Georgia's history and, at worst, deviated so far from the truth to be considered entirely fictional. Some would go as far as to make it seem like Georgia was just a vast, wall-less prison run by former inmates and criminals who thrived on anarchy and disorder. These misrepresentations may even lead people to think the prisons in Britain were overflowing so much that the only solution was to ship inmates off to other colonies in hopes of emptying the prisons. The reality of the situation is far simpler.

By and large, there were two motives behind the founding of Georgia:

1. The British government wanted to establish a military stronghold that buffered the other twelve colonies from the Spanish and native populations in Florida.
2. Some leaders in Parliament wanted to create a "safe haven" for debtors who were previously confined under corrupted pretenses in poorly kept prisons.

There were no boats full of hardened criminals crossing the Atlantic and no free-for-all New World colony to arrive at. Rather, men and women needing a second chance and the soldiers to keep them safe while they pursued that opportunity arrived in Georgia.

England vs. Spain

After the New World was discovered, a race began among the European giants to see who could conquer and acquire the most. Spain, still recovering from the shot to its ego after the defeat of the Spanish Armada in the 1580s, was looking to force England out of the fight for land and trade in the New World. The Spanish already had the upper hand as the sponsors of Columbus's original journey that led to the discovery of the Americas.

Using the routes discovered by Columbus and others, Spain began settling in modern-day Mexico and moved slowly upward. They claimed modern-day Texas, most of the Gulf Coast, and Florida (though they were often fending off native groups in Florida). They were also able to move west over time, laying claim to most of the American Southwest, California, and more.

As we already discussed, England had the Thirteen Colonies along the Atlantic coastline, in addition to a few islands in the Caribbean.

You can imagine that the expansive Spanish claim, along with their earlier discovery of the lands themselves, drove the English to jealousy. You can further imagine that when the English had finally established trade and cash-crop farming in the Carolinas (the two states north of Georgia) and noticed Spanish Florida pointing a big cannon at them, they were none too pleased.

And this was when Georgia stepped into the history books—as the punching bag of the Thirteen Colonies.

The Georgia Colony, named after King George II, was formally established in 1732; this was almost fifty years after the twelfth colony, Pennsylvania, was established and seventy years after South Carolina's founding in 1663. As we will see time and again, Georgia did things a little differently than the other colonies. Usually, after a group of people settled in the New World, they would apply with the English government to receive a formal charter. These charters were what made colonies *official*, and the colonies would set up a local governor to keep laws and establish order on behalf of the English government.

This was not so in Georgia.

Georgia was the first and only colony to be ruled by a group of overseers called the Board of Trustees. What made this a particularly interesting situation is that unlike the governors of other colonies, the Board of Trustees was seated in England, not Georgia. The most prominent founder of the board was John Oglethorpe, but we'll get to him in a minute.

The Board of Trustees struggled early on to have a clear and uncompromised vision for the new colony. The original charter was fraught with contradictions and was often ignored entirely. For example, the charter "explicitly banned [slavery] at the outset, along with rum, lawyers, and Catholics" and Jews.[7] However, when a group of Jewish settlers landed in 1733 (the same year Savannah was established), they were permitted to stay. In 1752, a governor was appointed for Georgia after the decline of the Board of Trustees' influence on Georgia. This decline was marked by the legalization of rum in 1742 and slavery in 1751. Governors ruled Georgia until 1776, the onset of the Revolutionary War.

English Prison Reform

English prisons in the 18th century were a far cry from the modern American prison system. Today, we see prisoners being given lodging and food during the duration of their sentence as an industry standard. However, the same was not the case before the prison reforms of the 1730s.

---

[7] Cobb, James and John Inscoe. "Georgia History."

Let us go over a brief run-down of how these prisons, called *gaols* at the time, were so cruel to debtors.[8] First things first, at this point in English history, employment was low. The jobless made up a large portion of the population. Without welfare systems in place to assist them, they would often go years or a lifetime without proper work. When a person was arrested, regardless of their employment status, they were held at the prison to await trial. This might sound familiar because that is also how the modern American system works unless an accused can make bail, but that's an entirely different conversation. However, the 18th-century British prisoner had to pay their own way. If they wanted to eat a meal while they awaited trial, they had to pay a fee. If they wanted to be let out of their shackles for a time, they had to pay a fee. If they needed any kind of service while in prison, they had to pay a fee.

Now, this may not be a terrible system if the average British prisoner was well-to-do, but we all know that was not the reality. To make matters worse, if a prisoner could not pay for the services or food they needed, it was simply put on their "tab." By the end of their trial, if they were found innocent, it came time to pay off their bill. However, if they could not afford to pay for all the services and food they had been given, guess where they would end up? That's right: back in prison!

With the rampant unemployment at the time, it is impossible to imagine (at least today) how this could ever have been the cycle endured by so many. It would have continued unrestrained were it not for James Oglethorpe, a soon-to-be member of the Georgia Board of Trustees. After the death of his friend, Robert Castell, from a preventable exposure to smallpox while in jail, Oglethorpe made it his pet project to find a solution to the debtor's prison problem.

As a member of Parliament, James Oglethorpe lobbied the ruling body to make changes to the present system. He was named the head of an investigative committee and was appalled at all they discovered. Apart from the "conditions, abuses, and extortions" faced by many prisoners, he was especially taken aback by the sheer number of British citizens who had been placed in jail for no reason apart from their debts.[9]

---

[8] Holzwarth, L. "The Reality of Debtor's Prisons in Britain and North America. History Collection, last modified Dec 8, 2022.

[9] Jackson, Edwin. "James Oglethorpe." New Georgia Encyclopedia, last modified Jul 21, 2020.

There had to be a better way.

While Oglethorpe's investigative committee was given the runaround, they were eventually able to amend some of the problems and corruption that had been exposed during the investigation. These efforts made Oglethorpe become something of a national star. However, he remained distressed that his prison reforms did little to actually solve the more systemic issue at the time: poverty and joblessness. Name recognition from his humanitarian efforts for the prison system would become his greatest weapon in creating a real solution to the problem: the founding of the Georgia Colony.

Oglethorpe and his colleagues believed that if they could enable the poor to have jobs in the New World, they would be able to relieve those families and individuals of the poverty they faced in England. The goal was to determine which individuals would be able to go to the new colony and obey the laws there. Georgia would not be home to run-of-the-mill prisoners (like is often portrayed); those whose lives would change dramatically for the better went there. Oglethorpe wanted to see debtors transformed into landowners, merchants, farmers, and tradesmen.[10]

With this vision, the Board of Trustees was formed, fundraising began, and Georgia was born.

However, Oglethorpe was not the only Englishman to use Georgia to make changes that would inevitably extend to the rest of the colonies.

Georgia and the Great Awakening

In 1735, when John Wesley and his brother Charles arrived in Georgia, they planned to use their time to evangelize Native Americans. Both Oxford graduates, the Wesley brothers were responsible for bringing what would later be called Methodism to the Americas. Their arrival was, unbeknownst to them, right as the First Great Awakening was beginning in America. The Great Awakening was a time in American history when religion—specifically Christianity—was on the rise. Through a series of leaders and events all across the colonies, beginning in Massachusetts with Jonathan Edwards, the people's faith was "awakening" after years of religious decline or apathy.

---

[10] Jackson, Edwin. "James Oglethorpe."

Out of Georgia, though, the second-most important leader of this transformative time in American history arose: George Whitefield.

George Whitefield, born in 1714 as the youngest of seven children to a few innkeepers near Bristol, England, went on to become arguably the most popular preacher of the 18th century and the first mass revivalist. Growing up, he would often retell what sermons he heard in the Anglican and Presbyterian churches in his hometown. This was an indication of his love for theater, performance, and oration, and this love would later draw him away from his studies at Oxford. However, theater and drama would remain essential parts of how he taught the Christian faith.

After receiving an inward calling toward ministry, Whitefield went on to be a servitor at Oxford beginning in 1732, where he joined in with the Wesleys' Methodism movement. Before leaving London to join the Wesleys in Georgia, Whitefield made a name for himself as a preacher in and around the city. During this time, he would often preach to those less likely to be found in a church: students, the poor, prisoners, and the illiterate—everyone was welcomed in his audience. When he took up the pulpit, religion had recently become a commodity. Preachers were competing with merchants and salesmen for "business." Religion was their ware, and attention was their price, and in Whitefield's case, he won out against the merchants. There could not have been a better time for the actor-preacher to take the stage.

In Georgia and the rest of the colonies, as time went on, he focused more on the invitation to experience new faith than he did on teaching doctrine; that was a role for other revival leaders. News of Whitefield spread by word of mouth, and crowds materialized out of nowhere when he traveled throughout the colonies.[11]

Once in Georgia, he adapted to the culture to reach its people (no matter how unpleasant he felt it was) and was quickly left by the Wesleys to run missions among Methodists from his new home base in Georgia. He was convinced it would be a difficult season, but outside the heat, he enjoyed his time. He was successful where the Wesleys were not. By being open to the customs of others and showing charity, Whitefield was able to open doors with folks the Wesleys were heavily persecuted by. It was also during this time that he began the Bethesda Orphanage, beginning his

---

[11] Stout, Harry S. *The Divine Dramatist: George Whitefield and the Rise of Modern Evangelicalism (Library of Religious Biography)*. Print, Pg. 37. September 9, 1991.

itinerant career so he could travel to raise funds to support it (his travels included London and the Thirteen Colonies)

After a stint in London, Whitefield returned to the colonies, starting in the north and moving down toward his new home in Georgia. He was able to amass a huge following near Philadelphia in part because of the printing done by his life-long friend Benjamin Franklin. Whitefield was very American in how he did things. He was available to all, preached outdoors, and was boosted by public opinion, which was positive thanks to the work of men like Franklin. The size of his crowds often exceeded the population of the towns themselves! His travels were also astonishing for that time, as he journeyed about 1,200 miles in all of 43 days. Most important, though, were not the lengths of his travels or the size of the crowds but the way he brought the colonies together.

Whitefield was able to unify them under one message, and as a result, he became a tangible figure for people to follow. Clergy, newspapers, books, and letters all spoke of his coming and grew his partnerships in the colonies, which led to smaller revivals that really allowed for the Great Awakening to happen in the first place. In all his preaching, he never took the stage from local ministers. Whitefield would preach during the week, never on a Sunday morning, and he never lost sight of his mission to see hearts transformed.

However, on both the American and London fronts, Whitefield had harsh critics. Whitefield and his comrades were often the targets of mob violence.

In 1741, he married Elizabeth James, and she began to run the Bethesda Orphanage in Georgia during his absence. For the next almost twenty years, Whitefield would spend time on both sides of the Atlantic (except for eight years spent in England due to sickness and war with France) doing what he did best: preaching, raising funds for the Bethesda Orphanage, and planning for the future.

The Georgia preacher had become an American icon.

Unfortunately for Whitefield, his sickness became worse during some college visits in the late 1760s. However, these college visits spurred in him an old longing to open his own college in the South, and he thought the orphanage would be a great starting place. He tried for years to create a college, although it would not be created until after his death.

Before his death in 1770, Whitefield did one last tour of the colonies. He was received as a hero and a spectacle everywhere he went, which was par for the course. Much of this time was spent on horseback, which was hard travel for the fifty-five-year-old Whitefield. Traveling was made worse because of his many colds and nighttime sicknesses. Whitefield's death was almost as widely mourned as and only outdone by George Washington. Even the famed poet Phyllis Wheatley created an elegy for him.

As America drew ever closer to war with England, many historians credit Whitefield with being a chief unifier of the Thirteen Colonies, making a war against the world's greatest military possible. Though Georgia might have been the youngest and least populated colony by the start of the Revolutionary War, one cannot help but imagine how things might have gone differently had Georgia not been home to "America's Preacher."

Chapter 3 – Georgia and the Revolutionary War

Unlike many northeastern colonists, Georgians were generally unsympathetic to the revolutionary spirit of the colonies.

Founded by the Board of Trustees for the purpose of providing some charity toward debtors, it is easy to see how Georgians would be inclined to see the British as their benefactors. While many colonists saw the government as over-taxers and repressors, first-time landowning Georgians who were former debtors saw the taxes being levied as a better alternative to debtor's prison. Under British rule, whether the Board of Trustees or the later appointed governors, Georgians prospered. There were schools, cash was flowing, families were thriving, and, above all, the British military kept the native tribes in Florida and the west from attacking the colonists. Even before the Native Americans were a direct threat, the military (then funded by Oglethorpe) built fortifications along the coastline to defend from would-be conquering Spaniards.

All in all, Georgia was arguably a better place under British rule than any other colony.

But not everyone saw it that way.

Georgia Can't Decide

After the First Continental Congress in Philadelphia in 1774, the delegates asked all the colonies to form an association. Their goal was to basically make British trade illegal in the colonies. As you may have already guessed, Georgian leaders were a bit leery. This can be seen by the fact that Georgia was the only colony that chose not to send a single delegate to the First Continental Congress.

With the call to join an association, a provincial congress gathered in Savannah, Georgia, on January 18th, 1775. The Provincial Congress of Georgia had two goals. First, it had to decide if joining the association and banning trade with the British would be a good thing. As you might imagine, the group was torn pretty cleanly in half about what to do next. *Are we sure we want to break ties with the British?*

The Provincial Congress of Georgia's second task was an easy one: select delegates to attend the Second Continental Congress in Philadelphia on May 10th, 1775. While the group did not have trouble deciding on the men who would represent the colony, those they selected all declined to go to Philadelphia because of the Provincial Congress of Georgia's inability to make a decision. Because of the group's inaction, the Parish of St. John (an Anglican church near Savannah) took matters into its own hands and sent Lyman Hall to the Second Continental Congress. Lyman Hall, acting in good faith, participated in all the Second Continental Congress debates, but he did not vote on any issues because he did not see himself as a representative for the entire state.

Interestingly enough, on May 11th, 1775, not even a full day after the Second Continental Congress gaveled its session to order, a group known as the Sons of Liberty broke into a powder magazine in Georgia's capital city (Savannah) and divided their winnings among themselves and South Carolina revolutionaries. These radical revolutionaries were empowered by the growing discord in Georgia about British rule. With news of Lexington and Concord (the first official battle of the Revolutionary War in which, supposedly, the British unintentionally fired on a column of militiamen) reaching the ears of the southernmost colony, many who had sympathized with the British had made up their minds: let the American Revolution begin.[12]

With the sentiments of their people changing, the Provincial Congress gathered for a second time on July 4th, 1775, to select and send delegates to the Second Continental Congress. These representatives would go on

---

[12] The Battles of Lexington and Concord are known for seeing the first shot of the war being fired. This shot was often called the "shot heard around the world" due to its impact on history. To this day, no one is sure which side fired first.

to sign the Declaration of Independence in 1776: Button Gwinnett, George Walton, and Lyman Hall.

Along with sending official delegates to Philadelphia, the Provincial Congress also implemented a plan to enact the ban on British trade. They did this through local committees throughout the state. These committees were mostly led by Whig-loyal (the revolutionary-aligned political "party" of the time, referred to by the British as traitors) farmers, merchants, and artisans in the local area.[13] This irritated the royally appointed governor James Wright, who thought these groups were incapable of governmental leadership.

Governor James Wright's view was, in small part, why the American Revolution began. His unwavering idea that the "everyday man" could not serve and lead in government was a sentiment felt across the entirety of colonial America. While it was harshest in Georgia, where the British government had more direct control of the government, it could be found elsewhere. Taxes, the historically identified "reason" for the revolution, were levied harshly without any representation of the colonial people in the British Parliament (hence, the revolutionary adage, "no taxation without representation"). By elevating these artisans and merchants to leadership, Georgia was already hinting at things to come, such as America's Georgia-born, peanut-farming future president.

Upon adjourning their gathering, the second Provincial Congress named a standing Council of Safety led by the would-be Declaration of Independence signer George Walton to maintain order and oversee those local committees.

War in Georgia

Division

Even before fighting began between the colonists and the British, some colonists in Georgia fought amongst themselves. Thomas Brown, founder of Brownsborough and a Loyalist, was on one side of the conflict, and on the other was the committee leaders.

Brown had come from Britain in 1774 to take some of the recently ceded lands the Georgia governor had advertised. With no deep ties to

---

[13] Those in the colonies who continued to support the British were known as Loyalists or Tories, while those opposed the British were called Whigs. However, in the colonies, Whigs were often referred to as Patriots, while in Britain, they were called "rebels" or even "traitors."

the colonies, his loyalties remained to the Crown. Brown was a very vocal dissenter of the association and the committees in Georgia that enforced its policies. When he was confronted, he refused to change his ways.

What followed was grim. His refusal sparked the Sons of Liberty to "[torture] him in various ways, scalping and fracturing his skull, burning his feet, and hauling him, unconscious, through the streets of Augusta as an object lesson to those who would denounce the Association."[14]

Surprisingly, Thomas Brown survived. And after his recovery, he was (understandably) very upset. After gathering other Loyalists from South Carolina, Brown threatened to march on Augusta, Georgia. What followed instead was a few skirmishes in northern Georgia before Brown and his followers sought aid in Florida. Their hope was to get a platoon of rangers and some Native Americans to march up with them from the south. Brown was refused and advised by several Loyalist governing officials to wait until the British army arrived to do anything else.

<u>Invasion</u>

After the theft of several crop transport ships and the rescue of Torrie Governor Wright by the British on March 2nd and 3rd, 1776 (in what became known as the Battle of the Rice Ships), the new acting government in Georgia attempted three separate invasions of Florida. This acting government was formed on May 1st, 1776, as a result of Governor Wright leaving the state.

The original fighting force was to be led by revolutionary General Charles Lee under the influence of the Georgia government. As major general of the South, Lee's intent was to lead Virginia's, North and South Carolina's, and Georgia's fighting forces into Florida to squash Brown and some of the Native American resistance there.

Unfortunately, Lee was called back to the north and took the Virginia and North Carolina militias with him. Without these two forces, South Carolina pulled back, leaving the Georgia militia (under the command of Lachlan McIntosh) to go it alone. Three separate attempts were made between 1776 and 1778 to invade eastern Florida. After the first two attempts and due to some political tensions, McIntosh was sent to Valley Forge to join George Washington's forces.

---

[14] Cashin, Edward. "Trustee Georgia, 1732-1752." New Georgia Encyclopedia, last modified Dec 10, 2019.

In his place, Georgia Governor John Houstoun led the militia on its third and final invasion attempt. While a contingent of the fighting force was able to drive out Brown and his men from a fort on the St. Marys River, little else was accomplished in Florida over the course of three years. If anything, it stirred up a little more animosity that led to some Native American troubles in the backcountry.

Constitution

While the botched Florida invasion was happening on the Georgia border, in the political backrooms, a new government was being formed.

After the establishment of the Rules and Regulation in May of 1776, a frame for government in the absence of a governor in the state, the Continental Congress recommended all the colonies form a permanent and lasting state constitution. Georgian representatives got to work quickly in October 1776. These elected representatives met in Savannah for the State Constitutional Convention.

The radical leaders were the most outspoken and ended up leading much of the direction of the convention. As a result, Georgia was able to have the most democratic government of any of the original colonies.

(A quick side note: When we say that Georgia had the most "democratic government," it is important that we do not impose our 21st-century perspective on this. At this time, the Democratic Party was not even a thought in anyone's mind. By saying it was "democratic," we mean that in the truest sense: democracy was at hand in Georgia. Without going into great detail about the nuances of government theory, let us say that when you hear "democracy" in its purest meaning, then every person in the electorate (which is the group that votes in elections) would get to vote. By saying that Georgia had the "most democratic" constitution, we mean to say that more people in Georgia got to participate in elections than anywhere else in the country.)

In most colonies, and later in the United States, only landowning white men were able to vote. The Georgia electorate would also include any white man over twenty-one who owned property, but the land had to be worth ten pounds. Georgia also allowed white men over twenty-one who were employed as artisans to vote, regardless of land ownership. This electorate was responsible for voting in members of the one-house assembly, which was responsible for enacting legislation and electing the governor, judges, and other state officials.

Enacted on February 5th, 1777, the new Georgia Constitution also established the first eight counties: Burke, Camden, Chatham, Effingham, Glynn, Liberty, Richmond, and Wilkes. Besides Liberty, each county was named after a parliamentarian in England who sympathized with colonial independence.

Restoration

As has been said several times already, things were different in Georgia, whether it was the natives, the colonists, or the constitution. Up to now, Georgia had set the pace for others or just run in its own lane as though no other colony existed.

It was time again for Georgia to be first.

In the north, the American Revolutionary War had come to a bit of a standstill. The British were making inroads to quell the war, and the colonies had run into a bit of a wall. With that realization in mind, British General Sir Henry Clinton in New York gave Lieutenant Colonel Archibald Campbell new orders. Clinton and others had been informed that there were many Loyalists in Georgia who were waiting to join the fight, so Clinton wanted Campbell to invade with his three thousand soldiers. The goal was to win back the territory and seats of power to restore Georgia to the British and set an example of restoration for the remaining colonies.

Here is how Cashin, an expert on the Georgian arm of the American Revolution, describes the initial invasion:

> "On December 28, 1778, Campbell's army landed unopposed on a bluff below Savannah, advanced through the swamps by an unguarded path, and overwhelmed General Robert Howe's defenders of Savannah. Campbell waited until January 12 for the arrival of Prevost's Royal Americans and Brown's Rangers from Florida, and on January 24 began a march with Brown's Rangers to Augusta in the backcountry. Except for a skirmish at the Burke County courthouse involving Brown's Rangers, Campbell was unopposed."

After taking possession of Augusta on January 31st, 1779, the southern invasion strategy seemed to be a complete success, bookended by Campell hearing that another 1,400 Loyalists in Georgia were marching to join him. However, more allies were cut off at Kettle Creek by South Carolinian forces; the battle that ensued is credited with keeping northern

Georgia free from British occupation.

On the same day as the Battle of Kettle Creek, Campbell left Augusta when he heard news that 1,200 North Carolina militia troops were marching his way. In a later battle on March 3rd, British Lieutenant Colonel James Mark Prevost turned upon the Americans and routed them at the Battle of Briar Creek. This battle would ensure the British controlled southern Georgia for the foreseeable future.

Three Governments

As the war waged in Georgia, the front was not the only place fighting was happening.

In a series of preventable and, to be honest, juvenile political blunders, Georgia ended up with two Whig governments in Augusta and a British royal regime in Savannah. It all started in June 1779 when an ad hoc committee was formed to try to make order out of the chaos in the midst of the war. Because the government of Georgia was adjourned from Savannah (where the British were in control), this committee gathered to set up a temporary replacement government in Augusta.

(**A quick side note:** One thing to remember about these historical political situations is that the governments of the states and, later, the nation operated a little differently than they do now. For example, in today's world (and for most of the last 150 years), travel to and from Washington, DC, is easy. Representatives hop on a plane, spend time in town writing legislation, vote, debate, discuss, and then head home after a few weeks. Then, after a little bit of time, they do it all over again. Back in the 18th and 19th centuries, this was not the case. Government members would spend weeks traveling to the capital, work for another few weeks, and head home. Like today, they would then go back and do it again (just with a bigger break).

This was the case in Georgia as well. By June 1779, government officials had either scattered due to the British invasion of Savannah or had adjourned already. Regardless of which category a member fell into, it would be a long time before they could be found, contacted, and prepared to head north to Augusta. In this desperate, leaderless moment, the thrown-together committee made a decision: to form a Supreme Executive Council that would lead before the next official session of the Georgia government. The Supreme Executive Council held its first meeting on July 24th and, in early August, elected John Wereat president.

As you might expect, this caused infighting, disagreements, and multiple governments.

Shortly after Wereat's presidency in the state began, he denounced the Georgia Constitution as too radical. This emboldened some of the more democratically radical leaders in Georgia to try and restore some order. By October 1779, Major General Benjamin Lincoln ordered George Walton to head down to Augusta and see that a proper election be held to form a working constitutional government. And he did. The assembly was elected, and they chose Walton as governor. Wereat and the Supreme Executive Council, to no one's surprise, refused to recognize Walton's election.

This same year, Governor Sir James Wright returned to Georgia. His arrival was at almost the same time the Supreme Executive Council was born: July 14th, 1779. With Wright returned, Georgia officially had its three governments. In Savannah, there were both a radical and a conservative Whig government, and in Augusta, there was a royally appointed regime. When Georgia was barely hanging on, it had three governments to try and rule it, which was not an ideal situation.

Siege at Savannah

Upon his return, Governor Wright officially announced that Georgia was "restored" to the Crown, meaning it was once again a British colony. This came with a perk: no taxation. In true Georgian fashion, Georgia was the one and only colony to have such an honor bestowed upon it (please note the sarcasm).

The celebration did not last long, though. In September, Count Charles Henri d'Estaing of France took his small fleet of twenty-five ships to the coastline of Georgia to do Washington a favor and try to recapture Savannah. With his army of four thousand to five thousand, d'Estaing began to besiege the city of Savannah. After thirteen days of the siege, on September 16th, d'Estaing demanded the surrender of Savannah. British General Augustine Prevost requested the French give him twenty-four hours before he made his decision; he was able to buy just enough time to allow Lieutenant Colonel John Maitland to come down from South Carolina with his eight hundred Redcoats to bolster the British forces in Savannah. Prevost, now emboldened and better prepared, declined to surrender.

Fast forward to October 9th, 1779, and the allied forces launched an assault upon the British. The invading colonists and French forces suffered 752 casualties, while the British defenders lost only 18 men and had 39 wounded. With this crushing defeat, the French returned to their ships, and the troops from South Carolina returned to the state.

With the victory in Savannah and other victories in South Carolina, the "rebellion" seemed to cool in Georgia. So much so that on July 10th, 1780, the Royal Council in Savannah declared that peace and restoration had come to Georgia. Little did they know that the revolution had just gone to hide in the mountains.

The War in Georgia Ends

June 5th, 1781, was the turning point that marked the end of the war in Georgia.

For almost an entire year, beginning with the siege of Savannah, there were several backcountry skirmishes between the colonial forces and the varied British leaders and their troops. One predominant leader was Lieutenant Colonel Thomas Brown, who commanded both regulars and native troops in Augusta. After repeated guerrilla-type skirmishes in the woods and hills of Georgia, a siege began in Augusta on May 22nd, 1781, with Brown trapped inside Fort Cornwallis (named for the British commander in the south). Three separate sets of colonial troops got ready to besiege the city.

After two weeks, a group of colonial engineers built a tower upon which to set a cannon. With the tower, the colonial army could point their cannon directly at Fort Cornwallis, leaving Brown no choice but to surrender the city on June 5th, 1781.

By August 17th, the official government of Georgia was able to gather again in Augusta and begin the hard work of recovering the government. Two big decisions were made by the restored legislature. Firstly, they elected Nathan Brownson governor for the remainder of 1781, and they also allowed General Nathanael Greene to establish a standing one-hundred-man and one-hundred-horse militia. Using these troops, Greene would wage a war of attrition against the British still in Savannah. By the next summer, Sir Wright was ordered to evacuate Savannah, and the remaining Loyalist army was defeated.

After years of loss and restoration, news that the preliminary peace treaty ending the Revolutionary War was signed reached Savannah in late May 1783.

Chapter 4 – Slavery in Georgia

After Governor Wright's initial departure in 1776, he and his Loyalist compatriots left behind many things, including their slaves. Over the next six years, raiding parties came up from Florida, colonists went south to attack the raiding parties, the British returned and sacked Savannah, and the colonists ultimately won the revolutionary conflict.

Granted, with the constant changing of hands every few years near the major cities and the general confusion that war brings, many slaves were able to escape. Some five thousand of the estimated fifteen thousand slaves in Georgia are thought to have escaped. Afterward, it is expected they did one of a few things. First, many went toward Savannah to try to form a new life in the city. Second, they may have gone off in search of family at other plantations. Third, groups of escaped slaves may have chosen to form their own small community in an isolated part of the coastline.

It cannot be overstated, however, that the approximately ten thousand slaves who remained were used as a form of currency as the war raged in Georgia. Some military leaders went as far as to pay soldiers part of their wages with slaves who were taken in raids or after battles. As is expected, many died in and around the battles or on the journey to their new "homes" after battles.

During the American and French attempt to sack Savannah, the British had local slave owners "donate" slave labor to construct fortifications in and around the city, which is not a terribly surprising choice. What was surprising at this time, however, was that the British went as far as to arm some slaves and place them in uniform. They even promised freedom to these fighters. It is important to note that the British might not have succeeded in the Battle of Savannah without the help of these soldiers.

For years to come, many black or former slaves worked hard to ensure their independence. To do so, some armed themselves in public, while others carried out their own enterprises and businesses that contributed to the community. Most important to the continued freedom and culture of the blacks in Georgia at the end of the rebellion was the formation of the Black Baptist denomination.

The Black Church of Georgia

Andrew Bryan, a former slave, helped found the First African Baptist Church in Savannah after converting under the preaching of George Liele some years after Bryan was moved to Georgia from South Carolina. After Liele's departure, Bryan took over the small congregation of slaves in Savannah. In 1788, Bryan was officially recognized by other (white) ministers and ordained as a Baptist pastor.

One of the things that put Bryan on the map for these other ministers to come to him was a reaction to a beating. Not long after Liele left, Bryan's brother Solomon also converted to the faith. As the two led their infant church, they were both beaten and imprisoned for their preaching.

(**A quick side note:** It was rather common for black church leaders to suffer in this way even into the Jim Crow period many years later. Later on, beatings or jail time would be under the guise of some other "crime" than preaching, but in the Antebellum period, many whites (especially white slave owners) saw blacks preaching as an empowering and dangerous act that might incite rebellion.)

However, the men's owner, Jonathan Bryan, intervened. He went to the authorities, secured the enslaved Bryan brothers their freedom, and earned some freedom for the black church movement as well. Jonathan even went as far as to provide a rice barn for Andrew Bryan to hold church gatherings in.

In 1794, Bryan purchased his and his family's freedom and began his own business. He continued to devote himself to the church as well. By 1802, First African Baptist Church had grown to host 850 members. Before his death in 1812, the church was steadily growing toward an unprecedented 2,795 members, which happened 20 years after his death.

Thanks to Andrew Bryan and others like him, the Black Baptist denomination was able to grow, and it still remains a central part of Georgian life today. It survived the Civil War, Reconstruction, and Jim Crow. It actually gained momentum along the way, which cannot be said of many other (and mostly white) Christian churches during those same periods. The Black Baptist Church has some doxological and ecclesiological differences from other evangelical groups that contributed to this momentum. It was described by Hayes, an African American church historian, as the following:

> "African 'survivals,' or fragments of African religion that have remained [in the teaching of the church], though in a different context. The music of Black Baptist churches contains cadences and rhythms of distinctly African origin, and the Black Baptist understanding of baptism as entry into the community can be traced to certain African rituals. The engagement of the churches in matters of politics and social justice can also be seen as a survival of the African religious view in which all life is sacred. Thus, in contrast to many white Baptists who have insisted on separating 'church and state,' Black Baptists have heralded emancipation as the 'Day of Jubilee,' planned protests and taught citizenship classes in their churches, and invoked religious imagery to give social activism a higher meaning, as exemplified in King's sermon 'I've Been to the Mountaintop.'"[15]

As we move forward, we will continue to see how the African American population of Georgia worked to remain seen and heard throughout the major movements of history. We will also see how their voices affected great change across the entire nation.

The Cotton Gin

Until 1793, the two major cash crops in the American South had been indigo and tobacco. Both had been planted since colonists first settled in the New World. Tobacco began all the way back in 1605 with the Jamestown settlement. The agricultural term "cash crop" is used to describe anything grown by farmers intended for sale or manufacturing rather than for local consumption. Most American cash crops were shipped to Europe, where it turned a rather handsome profit for everyone involved.

---

[15] Hayes, John. "African American Baptists." New Georgia Encyclopedia, last modified Jul 26, 2017.

The change that occurred in 1793 saw a shift from a regional dependence on the two cash crops to an overabundance of just one: upland cotton. While the other type, sea island cotton, was already being grown in and around Georgia, it was not as popular for textile production.

During Eli Whitney's stay at the late Nathanael Greene's home (Greene had already died a revolutionary hero, and his wife Catharine ran the plantation), he learned of the struggle of harvesting upland cotton. An inventor by hobby and tutor by trade, Whitney, who was from Massachusetts, came to Georgia to tutor a local family. Upon his arrival, he saw that the job had been given to someone else, and far from home and cashless, he accepted the widowed Mrs. Greene's offer to stay with her family. One evening, when a few local farmers came for dinner, Whitney learned of their plight. Unlike its sea island cousin, upland cotton was notoriously difficult to separate fiber from seed. Having to do so by hand took enormous effort and time. Ever the inventor, he offered to find a solution.

By late 1793, Whitney had done it: the cotton gin was born. What would typically have taken a few slave workers all day could now be done by one in a few hours. The production of cotton rapidly expanded. "In 1801 planters produced 48 million pounds of cotton as compared with just 2 million pounds a decade earlier. By the eve of the Civil War, the South's cotton production exceeded a billion pounds annually."[16] This exponential increase had two impacts on America moving forward.

First, the Northern states saw a massive uptick in their production. The South, historically, is where the dominant share of cash crop growth occurred, and for good reason: more land was available in the South than in the smaller, denser states of the northeast, and the climate was more temperate due to warmer winters. As cotton production in the South grew, the North ended up growing textile mills (factories) to keep up with the production. The cotton gin, by extension, did just as much good for the Northern economy as it did the South. Because the production of cotton clothing and goods increased, so did its availability to the public; it was no longer available to just the wealthy. The farmers who grew the crop were actually able to afford and have access to the product.

---

[16] Hatfield, Edward. "Eli Whitney in Georgia." New Georgia Encyclopedia, last modified Oct 31, 2018.

The second and more heartbreaking reality of the cotton gin was the equally exponential increase of slave labor in the South. To supply and run the cotton gin with enough raw cotton, plantations needed hundreds of working hands. As the demand for cotton grew, so did the South's dependence on enslaved people to complete the work. This part of the country later became known as the Black Belt because of the high concentration of slaves working the cotton fields. It expanded over time to include South Carolina, Alabama, Mississippi, and central and south Georgia.

(**A (not so) quick side note:** One of the tragic ironies of the Black Belt was that it grew dominantly because of the need for the materials to feed the growing textile industry of the North. It was a vicious cycle. The South increased cotton production, so barons in the North opened more factories. Then, farmers produced more cotton, and the North hired more workers and built more factories, resulting in the South growing more cotton to fill the factories, and the cycle went on. The irony is that as tensions soared about whether to keep or abolish slavery, the whole country was still wearing cotton clothing. There were many working in textile factories. And even though people were calling for an end to slavery at the end of the Antebellum period, they were not doing much to stop the need for slavery. Now, this is in no way an endorsement of slavery but rather a critique of how the country sought change. Something similar is happening today. Statistics would say that, all around the world, there are women and children working in sweatshops or dangerous factories who are not making close to a living wage, yet most buy the cheap clothing they produce.)

Whitney's Battle

After Eli Whitney sold a few of his early cotton gins, he returned to New England to file a patent for his newest invention and begin production. However, court battles ensued because of rip-offs and replications. The cost of all the court fees to fight the patent issue was more than Whitney had coming in from cotton gin production. Eventually, he gave in and just did what he could without his patent.

When the relationship between the US and France grew tense, with the country fearing conflict, Whitney saw it as an opportunity. By contacting the Secretary of the Treasury, Whitney was able to secure a contract to produce muskets for the military. While no armed conflict occurred, Whitney profited from the contract. He also created another new invention. By using the uniformity system (producing products that are all the same and use the same parts), he was able to create muskets that had interchangeable parts. This allowed for the guns to be repaired, not just replaced. This was a great leap in the manufacturing industry, which would gain popularity soon enough.

While there is certainly a longer conversation that could be had about slavery in Georgia and even about how elements of it still exist today, we will chat more about human rights and the changes that were needed a little later. In most ways, Georgia was different from its neighbors. However, slavery is one issue in which there was great uniformity in the South. Changes would come, though.

Chapter 5 – Antebellum Georgia

Apart from Whitney's cotton gin, there were several other things that happened between 1790 and the early rumblings of the Civil War in the 1850s. While none of the following occurrences are entirely earth-shattering, they still helped to pave the way for both the Civil War and Georgia's Reconstruction period.

Yazoo Land Fraud

Lamplugh, a Georgia historian, would say that the Yazoo land fraud was one of the "most significant" occurrences in Georgia between the American Revolution and the Civil War. In the end, it helped to change both the literal and the political landscape of Georgia.

The Yazoo land, named for the river that occupied it, was the far west territory claimed by Georgia. This would later become parts of Alabama and Mississippi. After the Revolutionary War, Georgia was struggling to defend and maintain this portion of the territory, so the state legislature began to seek ways to off-load the lands. After failing to cede the land to Congress in 1788, they began to search for companies willing to pay in gold and silver for the land.

On January 7th, 1795 (almost fifteen years after the state government began looking to sell), a deal was struck to sell thirty-five million acres in western Georgia to four separate companies for $500,000. Governor George Mathews signed the Yazoo Act, which successfully completed the sale.

There was a catch, however.

For the sale to go through successfully, a few people needed to be convinced of the deal's value. This was made possible by actually giving the money from the sale to those participating in the deal! James Gunn, the US senator from Georgia (not the famous movie director), was the one helping to move things along. He arranged for the $500,000 from the sale to be distributed to influential Georgians, including state legislators, other state officials, and newspaper editors. The money did not go into the bank for the state of Georgia to use, just the pockets of its politicians—it is crazy enough to sound like the plot of a bad heist movie.

As you might imagine, people were none too pleased about the sale, and many Georgians began to cry for a cancellation of the sale and signed several petitions to end it. Regardless, the sale went through, and the Yazoo land was gone.

It is worth mentioning that at this point in the national political landscape, there were two dominant political parties: the Federalists and the Jeffersonian Republicans (often called Democratic-Republicans). The Federalists, as their moniker suggests, tended to support legislation that gave the national (or the federal) government more control or power over the country. Democratic-Republicans favored legislation that supported a state's power. Senator Gunn was a Federalist, while Georgia's other senator, James Jackson, was a Democratic-Republican.

Jackson began a campaign to overturn the Yazoo sale and see the corruption ousted. As a Democratic-Republican, it is entirely expected that Jackson would not support the sale for, as we said before, it was not a popular sale among the people of Georgia.

In order to see his ends met, Jackson actually resigned his Senate seat and returned to Georgia to use the county court system and newspapers to gain an overwhelming number of seats in the state legislature. From there, he and his allies wrote the 1796 Rescinding Act, which came after Jackson held hearings to confirm the corruption charges of those involved in the original sale. The Rescinding Act nullified the Yazoo sale and was signed by the governor. Jackson went as far as to destroy records of the original sale and made sure those officials involved with the sale did not win reelection.

After buying time for the Democratic-Republicans to gain control of Congress, in 1802, Jackson and his allies successfully transferred the Yazoo lands to the United States for $1.25 million with the provision that the US would end any Native American claims to the land.

In 1810, the United States Supreme Court ruled the Rescinding Act unconstitutional and ensured the original purchasing companies in the Yazoo land sale received $5 million from another land sale in 1814.

Two things came as a direct result of the botched Yazoo land sale. First, Democratic-Republicans used the original sale as a political weapon for most of the next two decades, ruthlessly leveraging it against their opponents. More tragically, because Congress attained the land under the agreement to settle Native American claims, the Cherokee were sent along the Trail of Tears. In the midst of this tragedy, Georgia became the only southern state to be challenged in court about native land sovereignty in the US Supreme Court case *Worcester v. Georgia*.

Georgia Gold Rush

There are many anecdotes that tell tales of gold being discovered in Georgia. Whether rocks were kicked or creek beds were explored, there is no certainty about when gold was truly first discovered in Georgia. All that matters, though, is that it was.

The first documentation of the discovery of gold took place in the *Georgia Journal* of Milledgeville, Georgia, on August 1st, 1829, and is quoted below:

> "GOLD.—A gentleman of the first respectability in Habersham County, writes us thus under date of 22d July: 'Two gold mines have just been discovered in this county, and preparations are making to bring these hidden treasures of the earth to use.' So it appears that what we long anticipated has come to pass at last, namely, that the gold region of North and South Carolina, would be found to extend into Georgia."[17]

The discovery of gold helped to build up Georgia's economy, as well as change some of its geography, as "rushers" attempted to extract as much gold as they could. As we will see, miners rushing to northern Georgia created new settlements and bolstered old ones, which began to be another thorn in the side of the Native American tribes in the area.

Great Intrusion

The areas in which gold was discovered were soon flooded with people. Northern Georgia, known at that time as the Cherokee Nation,

---

[17] Originally published Aug 1st, 1829, in the *Georgia Journal* of Milledgeville, GA.

had an influx of thousands of gold rushers. Another newspaper reported that the Yahoola Creek had at least four thousand men panning it for gold by 1830.

The rush of gold seekers into the Cherokee Nation was known, even then, as the Great Intrusion. And with good reason. The white Georgians moved into the Cherokee Nation in search of riches; they paid no mind to whose land they were on. The more the Cherokee raised complaints, it seemed the more and more gold rushers could settle.

By 1832 and 1833, boomtowns had begun to spring up all across northern Georgia. The Auraria settlement had at least one thousand residents, while Dahlonega (the county center named after the Cherokee word for "golden") had one thousand residents, with an additional five thousand scattered in the immediate countryside.

Mining Operations

As the gold rushers came in, most were only able to afford the simplest mining technique: placer mining. They would find a promising spot, and using their shovel and a pan (a wide, shallow bowl), they would sift some river silt to see if it might potentially have a gold deposit nearby. David Williams, a Georgian historian, describes how this is possible by expanding on the meaning of "placer mining" to refer to "gold that has washed down from the hillsides and collected along mountain streams. When miners found a location that showed "good color," they set up camp and began working the area in earnest. A variety of tools were used to wash these deposits and extract the fine gold particles. The river bottoms were very attractive places to search for gold; miners frequently drifted flatboats into [the rivers] and dredged up rich sand and gravel."[18]

River dredging would occur after larger deposits had been discovered by pan nearer to the river's edge. It did sometimes require a team of miners, which was not an uncommon sight.

Place mining and teamwork for river dredging were popular among the majority of the miners because they did not require much start-up cost. Most of the gold rushers did not have a lot of capital, which is exactly why they came to seek their fortune in the first place. However, the more and more miners that arrived, the more the towns grew; the more that the towns grew, the more money became available to invest in hard-rock

---

[18] Williams, David. "Gold Rush." New Georgia Encyclopedia, last modified Sep 12, 2018.

mining. Since heavier equipment was needed for mining veins, instead of just a shovel and a pan, it could get rather expensive.

Hard-rock mining is similar to what you might picture when we say "mining." They would dig tunnels braced by rafters to avoid cave-ins and bring out rock and ore containing gold to be processed in something called a stamp mill. Each mill was different, both in capacity for ore and simplicity, with the largest able to run off water wheels near the river.

Mining Effects

One problem that was highlighted in this region at this time was the difficulty in valuing gold. In the Carolinas and Georgia, where gold veins were discovered, many merchants demanded immediate payment in cash or gold. It was often merchants who assigned value to the gold, which created a problem. The solution that locals came up with was to request a US Mint be established in the region to mint gold coins from the raw materials mined there. When miners could get coins from their gold, they would be able to have a consistent valuation of the material and keep that power out of the hands of merchants.

The petition succeeded, and in 1838, the Federal Branch Mint at Dahlonega (one of the first in the country) was established. In the first year alone, $100,000 worth of gold was minted; by 1861, when it closed, it had printed a total value of over $6 million (or close to 1.5 million individual coins).

It was also at this time that tensions between miners and natives grew. If we are being honest, it may be more accurate to say "between *Georgians* and natives," as many years of disagreement came to a head. For almost the first thirty years of the 19th century, the state government of Georgia had been holding lotteries to give away land that had been seized from the Cherokees and Creeks. With the establishment of the US Mint, there was a lot of prosperity in the northern area of Georgia, but none of it was for the Cherokees. The US Army eventually intervened to remove the Cherokee from the land in a tragic event known as the Trail of Tears.

Not more than eleven years after the *Georgia Journal* ran its "GOLD" article, most of the hard rock veins and river panning began to dry up or became too difficult to work with. With the inability to make a living, many considered the rush in Georgia to be over. As announcements of gold in California came in, many gave up on Georgia gold and headed west.

Higher Education

During Georgia's Antebellum period, two universities were chartered, both of which are still hosting classes today.

University of Georgia

The University of Georgia (UGA) was chartered in 1785. A Yale graduate, Abraham Baldwin, firmly believed that education should be available to more of the citizenry than it had been. He made this claim on the basis that an educated society was essential to maintaining a free government. Larry Dendy, a historian, summarized Baldwin's view by saying "that government has a responsibility to see that its citizens receive an education, and that all people—not just the wealthy and privileged—have a right to education."[19] It goes without saying, but once again, Georgia was shaking up the status quo. The University of Georgia was the first state-chartered school; no other state had a state-run university at this point. This established the framework for future state colleges and universities all around the country.

Even though the University of Georgia was charted shortly after the Revolutionary War, it took another sixteen years before anything really happened for the university.

Originally, state-designated lands were going to be used for the school, but with the pressure of running a brand-new state government, the legislature and governor's office let the land be used for other things. In 1801, John Milledge, a legislator, bought and donated about 633 acres to be used by the university. Classes began in September of that year and were taught by the only faculty member (who was also the university president), Josiah Meigs.

In 1806, the first permanent structure was built on the land donated by Milledge. Named for the founding father, the Franklin College building was often used as a misnomer for the university; for many years, it was called Franklin College rather than the University of Georgia. To honor this common error, as the liberal arts and science schools rose up, they named that division of classes the Franklin College of Arts and Sciences.

The Franklin College of Arts and Sciences was the only educational division to exist for many years until 1859 due to financial struggles at the university. In 1859, on the verge of the Civil War, the School of Law was

---

[19] Dendy.

started and then closed, along with the entire university, for two years during the Civil War.

Avoiding bankruptcy became possible during Reconstruction in 1872 when the University of Georgia was designated a land-grant recipient by the federal government. Thanks to the Morrill Act, they received the land and were taken with teaching agricultural and mechanical arts. This legislation helped the university to solidify its mission to be a public servant and see Georgia thrive.

The 20th century brought even more changes to the university. Before 1920, schools for education, business, forestry, pharmacy, home economics, and journalism, as well as graduate schools, were all started at UGA. Women were admitted regularly in 1918, and in January of 1961, UGA officially integrated when two African American students transferred in from a school in Atlanta.

In 1985, the University of Georgia became the first public higher education institution to celebrate its bicentennial in America. This was a year used by university leadership to raise funds to open more resources and arts centers throughout the university's network of schools.

Since that time, UGA has continued to grow and thrive, adding several new programs, campuses, and public service programs.

Georgia Wesleyan College

"Forever first for women's education—striving for excellence, grounded in faith, and engaged in service to the world" is Wesleyan College's mission.

Antebellum Georgia, like other portions of the nation, was marked by social reform movements spearheaded by young women. They led campaigns against slavery, alcohol, and poor prisons, all of which led these young ladies to consider themselves the equals of men. As a result, they began calling for even more reform. They believed they deserved opportunities that men got, so they focused on the creation of educational institutions for women that would offer an education and course load like men's colleges.

On July 8th, 1835, a group of Macon businesses met to raise funds to open the college. All members of the Methodist Church, they hoped to affiliate the school with their church. By the following January, the Methodist Conference voted to adopt the forthcoming college, and in December, the state chartered the Georgia Female College, making it the first degree-granting women's college in the world! Do I need to say that Georgia was leading the way, or is that just expected now? It was not until 1843 that the Methodist Church assumed any direct responsibility for the school and renamed it Wesleyan Female College.

A great deal of excitement came in January 1839 when the college opened its doors. With a first class of 168 women, the Georgia Female College was already rivaling most other state-sponsored schools in the South. The college was especially popular because it offered actual college courses rather than the high-school level classes that other schools tried to pass off as women's education. At Georgia Female College, the students were instructed in philosophy, history, and ancient and modern languages, along with other subjects. They also had the opportunity to earn the equivalent of a bachelor's degree.

Among many other firsts, like the establishment of the precursor to the sorority system and the first alumni association for Georgia liberal arts, Georgia Female College boasted two rather impressive firsts. "Women from Wesleyan include the first in Georgia to receive a Doctor of Medicine degree and the first to argue a case before the Supreme Court of Georgia."[20]

Unlike UGA, Wesleyan Female College remained open during the Civil War and even saw an uptick to 350 enrolled shortly afterward. By the early 20th century, they dropped "female" from the name and became Wesleyan College, named for the founder of Methodism in America, John Wesley, who originally came to Georgia. In 1919, the school received endorsements from the Southern Association of Colleges and Schools, an important accreditation body that still exists and still endorses Wesleyan College today. The school grew and strengthened, allowing it to survive the Great Depression and World War Two and benefiting from the economic growth following both. Before the 1970s, the university boasted an enrollment of around seven hundred women until women's colleges became viewed as antiquated during the women's movement. Since then, however, a revival in the popularity of such schools has led to enrollment going back up.

---

[20] Huff, Christopher. "Wesleyan College." New Georgia Encyclopedia, last modified Apr 30, 2019. https://www.georgiaencyclopedia.org/articles/education/wesleyan-college/.

Railroads

The development of rail lines in South Carolina is actually what initiated Georgia businessmen to lobby the legislature to charter a new railroad system and canal development company. The businessmen realized very quickly that building canals near the Savannah River was far more limited than just sticking to railroads, so in 1835, they got to work on the Central Rail Road of Georgia. This central line would grow over the years to be a 190-mile-long track to Macon.

The other important rail systems that were being built would run from Augusta to Athens and another from Macon to Forsyth. As time went on, the Georgia Railroad Company (though it would change names a few times) moved to Augusta; shortly afterward, it would have lines running to Marthasville, what would later be known as Atlanta.

Private railroads were not the only type in Georgia, though. The state chartered the Western & Atlantic Railroad (W&A) that linked to the Tennessee and Ohio Valleys. By building and opening this rail line, the state was able to connect trade hubs in Chattanooga, Tennessee, to what would later be Atlanta. Shortly thereafter, a fourth rail line linked to the other rail lines in Atlanta.

With all of these lines coming together in Atlanta, the city became a hub for trade in the American South. Once the Civil War began, Atlanta became a target of the North to reduce the South's ability to move troops, supplies, and other important goods to Confederate groups.

Over time, especially into the early 20th century, several of these rail lines were consolidated and linked with others throughout the South and mid-Atlantic regions. By that time, Georgia could boast more rail miles than any other state in the South. Today, the strong system in Georgia has a total of five thousand miles of rails connecting two major networks and several short lines.

Without Georgia and the development of its rail system, the Civil War would have likely been over long before the surrender at Appomattox. However, the rail system was not Georgia's only contribution to the bloodiest and deadliest war in American history. As we spoke about before, the advent of the cotton gin was a key impetus for many plantations to expand operations and their slave capacity. In the South, many believed that if one were to relinquish slavery, their livelihood would be threatened. You may imagine that the growing black church would have opened the eyes of many Georgians to the equity that could be had between black and white, yet while the church grew, so did the hold of slave owners over where their slaves went and when.

The Civil War, but more specifically the close of the Antebellum period, has more complexities and nuances than you may imagine, especially since the South has so often been cast as a unified mind rather than a group of separate states looking out for their own interests. Georgia always does things differently, as we will see again shortly, but some things might have been done to Georgia this time around that were far out of its control.

Chapter 6 – Civil War and Reconstruction

Georgia played a rather crucial role in the events immediately leading up to the succession crisis while also continuing to be the unique state we have come to know it as.

(**Disclaimer:** While the history of Georgia is permanently entwined with that of the rest of the Deep South and the Civil War, this work does not aim to give a full picture of the events or happenings of the Civil War apart from those that directly affected Georgia. Even then, our aim is not to detail all the events but rather those that helped to propel Georgia into the Reconstruction era and played a role in shaping Georgia forever.)

Secession

Due to the construction of the railroads throughout the early 1800s, Georgia had become a trading hub. Georgia's access to the ocean and seabound trade played in its favor as well, and it was the only Deep South state with a strong economy. Georgia had even come to be known as the Empire State of the South since its industrial economy grew. What is interesting, though, is that Georgia's economy, unlike the rest of the Deep South, was not entirely dependent on slavery. As has been recounted in many other works, the results of the Civil War decimated the economies of the former Confederate States because of their dependence on slavery. Georgia was diversified enough to have at least one leg to stand on after the war.

Georgia's "diversified portfolio," if you will, stems from the fact that it had two rather large geographical areas in which slavery was almost nonexistent: in the southeast, where wiregrass and longleaf pines grew, and in the northern mountains. In the Wiregrass, where trees dominated the landscape, there was some agriculture but nothing like the neighboring cotton- and rice-growing regions. Because of this, it was a comparably poorer part of the state and was often looked down upon by the more elite white landowners. A reason it was not readily farmed was because of fears of natives in the "wild" portions of the area, particularly those parts that could not be readily traversed due to the pine groves. The work that was done centered around cattle or other pastoral duties. The whips used by the herdsmen of the area had a tip that made a particular cracking sound. Since the population of the area was often looked down on by the elites, people came up with the derogatory term "cracker" for the stereotypical poor white cattlemen of the region.

Even so, Georgia still had the largest population of enslaved people and slave owners of any state in the South, second only to Virginia before its split into Virginia and West Virginia in 1863, which also made Georgia the largest state east of the Mississippi.

All of this, as you may imagine, made selecting delegates for the 1861 Georgia Secession Convention rather difficult. The slave-holding and non-slave-owning diversity in Georgia led to divided groups of delegates attending the secession convention. These people also held diverse opinions as a whole on the issues of slavery and secession. The delegates and those who voted for them at the polls in the months following the Lincoln election ranged from seeking immediate secession from the Union to staying the course with the Union and seeking cooperation with the federal government. In the end, a majority of those delegates voted to secede, and on January 19th, 1861, Georgia became the fifth state to leave the Union. By March of that year, the delegates had reconvened to ratify the new Confederate Constitution and to finalize a new state constitution for Georgia. It was only a few weeks later, on April 12th, that the first shots of the Civil War were fired from a cannon at Fort Sumter, South Carolina.

Georgian Confederates

Several notable leaders within the Confederate government hailed from Georgia. The Confederate Convention in February of 1861, where the constitution for the Confederate States was drafted, was organized in Montgomery, Alabama, by Howell Cobb. His brother, Thomas R. R.

Cobb, was a primary author of the Confederate Constitution and would later contribute heavily to the state constitution as well.[21] Thomas Cobb was actually one of the foremost legal minds in antebellum Georgia and one of the loudest voices to advocate for slavery and secession. He was such a profound legal mind that he published fifteen volumes of state Supreme Court reporting between 1851 and 1861 and contributed heavily to state codes. He would go on to be a brigadier general for the Confederate forces until his death at the Battle of Fredericksburg in 1862. Howell Cobb, before secession, had a rather illustrious career as well, serving in Congress for thirteen non-consecutive years, Speaker of the House for one term, governor for two years, and secretary of the treasury until Lincoln's election.

Another notable Georgian leading the Confederate government was Secretary of (Confederate) State Robert Toombs. As a public servant for four decades, Toombs spent almost his entire career in the Georgia Senate or the United States Senate as a staunch unionist. He devoted years to ensuring reconciliation between national and sectional interests. He even stood with Howell Cobb as a supporter of Henry Clay when he tried to calm secessionists in 1850. It is shocking then to see Toombs be a supporter and leader of the Confederacy. Strangely and perhaps a bit disappointing, there was no moment, event, or policy that caused Toombs to "switch sides" from unionist to secessionist. Rather, throughout the 1850s, he simply became disenfranchised with the efforts to hold things together and was won over by more radical members of his party. After Georgia's secession in 1861 in response to the Lincoln election, Toombs felt it was the right time to resign his Senate seat.

(**A quick side note:** What happened with Toombs is more common in American politics than we may imagine. Many elected officials have moderate and cooperative leanings when it comes to policy creation and leading the country. However, as the more "radical" (to use antebellum language) members of governing bodies gain power or volume in the debate and win the hearts of the constituents as a result, it becomes harder for the Toombses of the world to keep on their feet. For those moderate, cooperative representatives, having to fight in both directions, both with the opposing party and their own party, becomes too much, and we see them concede to the radical viewpoint of their party.)

---

[21] Cobb, James and John Inscoe. "Georgia History."

The Civil War in Georgia from the Perspective of Joseph E. Brown

The wartime governor of Georgia was Joseph E. Brown. Brown had entered the political arena in Georgia in only 1857 but quickly became an incredibly popular leader and champion of the common white man. After reelection in 1859, Brown, a Democrat, became a devoted voice for secession. His position was so intense that he called for the seizure of a federal fort before the legislature had officially voted for secession. Some historians believe that Brown's leadership and advocacy to secede was the thing that tipped the scales because Georgia was originally inclined to stay in the Union.

As governor, Brown only called for the strengthening of the Georgia militia in preparation for battle. However, in 1861, when the Confederate government was drafting troops for the unified war effort, Brown stood opposed to the growing power the centralized Confederate government had. Brown would often exempt men from being conscripted to Confederate service. There was a long and drawn-out struggle between Brown and Confederate President Jefferson Davis, which gave courage to other state leaders to push back on the draft as well. As Brown began to lose the fight with Davis, he turned his attention to home. If he could not keep soldiers from the battlefield that others chose for them, then he would support their families as best he could.

During Brown's second term, he established a form of welfare that primarily provided for the families of soldiers but also supported civilians who were victims of increasing inflation. The primary thrust of the welfare system was to provide these families and individuals with salt for the preservation of meat. As the war dragged on and more and more men were sent off to fight, more and more families were in need of aid from the Georgia government. To keep supplies up, Brown levied higher taxes on the rich. With all of this in mind, voters gladly reelected him to office in 1863.

As the war dragged on, so did Brown's opposition to Jefferson Davis and the rest of the Confederate leadership. On any occasion he could, Brown would loudly and publicly criticize the pitfalls and failings of the war efforts, such as the Confederate attempts to force goods out of Georgia, the attempted martial law to seize the Western and Atlantic Railroad, taxes, blockade running in the Atlantic, the call to conscript slaves late in the war with the promise of freedom, and more. As time went on, Brown even became friends with people from the Confederacy, like Toombs and Vice President Alexander Stephens. Unfortunately for Brown and the rest of the Confederacy, his criticisms, which were echoed by other state leaders, did nothing to empower or improve the war efforts. As Union General William T. Sherman marched across northern Georgia in a campaign that would ultimately be the "beginning of the end" of the Civil War, it became clear that the chain of command was not efficient enough to save Georgia. As Atlanta fell and Sherman began his burning March to the Sea, Brown called for peace.

Before we jump into the postwar era of Georgia, it would feel incomplete not to finish Governor Brown's story. After the war, he, like most other Confederate leaders, was arrested and briefly served a prison sentence in Washington, DC, before being paroled. Upon returning to Georgia, he supported the Reconstruction plan of President Andrew Johnson and was pardoned in September 1865. After joining the Republican Party, Brown was appointed to the state Supreme Court as chief justice, a post he served for two years. After Reconstruction, Brown rejoined the Democratic Party and opened a mining operation in northern Georgia. Using the state's convict release system, Brown earned large amounts of wealth. In this system, businesses could lease out the labor to convicts from prisons; at this time, many of those convicts were black men imprisoned on weak charges. With the work of these convicts, who were treated no better than slaves, Brown's operation boomed. He served in the Senate from 1880 to 1890 until he grew too ill to serve. After his death in 1894, his mining operation was investigated and found to have mistreated and neglected all of his leased workers.

With the Civil War at an end, the South, including Georgia, would have to rehabilitate to be considered for reentry into the Union. Georgia would again be seen as the one to shake the status quo.

Reconstruction

The Reconstruction era was a time of deep-seated political strife and tension, a time of struggle for balance between the states and the federal government, and of painful and dark racial violence.

Before we dive into the Reconstruction process, this is a good time to highlight some of the nuances of the political arena in the late 1800s. By this time in history, both major political parties had evolved, rebranded, shifted, or split. Beginning in the Jacksonian era (which was about ten presidents before Johnson), there was a sharp division in the Democratic-Republicans that led to what historians call the "second party system."

Now, this is not a book on political history, but let's look at the highlights of how this led to Reconstruction. When the Democratic-Republicans split, the new Democratic Party of Andrew Jackson stood for the sovereignty of the people and was supported by many lower-class or farming communities. The Whig Party, which would later rebrand itself as the Republican Party, stood on a platform of constitutionalism and fighting tyranny. By the Civil War, the third-party system was in place. Everything centered on slavery. Republicans opposed slavery, supported the freedmen (former slaves), and advocated for national banks, high tariffs, and some social spending. The Democrats, to put it bluntly, opposed the Republicans and everything they stood for. With the war fresh on everyone's mind, many dug their heels in and remained in these patterns until the 1890s.

Immediate Changes

With Governor Brown's arrest immediately after the Civil War ended, there was a chance of chaos erupting all across the state.

This was in part because of General William Sherman's March to the Sea. The state had been razed by the war. Apart from major cities being physically destroyed and family homes burned to the ground, the people were feeling destroyed. Since the beginning of the war, an estimated forty thousand Georgians had either been killed or purposefully dispersed in the aftermath of the war. The white population of the state was reduced to 590,000, while the new population of freed people was more than 460,000, a ratio of almost one to one.

Johnson Reconstruction, 1865-1866

After the assassination of Abraham Lincoln, whose Reconstruction plan, which aimed to give high levels of support to the newly freed people, was never implemented, Vice President Andrew Johnson, a Democrat, was inaugurated. He quickly established a provisional governor in Georgia. James Johnson was a unionist who had chosen to abstain from the war efforts in his native Georgia. One of the first things Governor James Johnson oversaw as a part of President Andrew Johnson's Reconstruction plan was to oversee elections for new constitutional convention delegates. One provision of Andrew Johnson's (and Lincoln's) Reconstruction plan was to have at least 10 percent of the state's population swear renewed loyalties to the Union and then form a new constitution.

The voters in the delegate election of 1865 numbered only 50,000 loyal adult white men; in the prewar elections in Georgia, 107,000 had voted. This means that a large percentage of the voting population, even when you factor in lives lost to the war, was not ready to swear loyalty to the Union after the Civil War ended. The new governing documents, like the one planned in October 1865 in Georgia, had to repeal any official Ordinance of Secession, abolish slavery, and "[repudiate] the Confederate debt."[22] In Georgia, the only other alterations from the original constitution were the prohibition of interracial marriage (one step toward what would come to characterize the Reconstruction in the South) and a new limit on the governorship: governors would now only be able to serve two two-year terms.

With a new constitution in place, Georgians could now establish a state government and elect congressional representatives. Election day was November 15th, 1865, and although the voting requirements were not as strict as they were earlier in the year for constitutional delegates, only thirty-eight thousand votes were cast. Those thirty-eight thousand voters elected a new governor, federal congressmen, and state legislators. Unionists were not often voted for, and Georgia elected many ex-Confederates to all of the needed positions. It is important to note, however, that most of these new leaders, like the new governor, Charles Jones Jenkins, did not originally support secession and had been pardoned after the war.

By December of that year, Georgia's General Assembly voted to ratify the Thirteenth Amendment. With slavery officially ended and Georgia returned to the Union, President Johnson handed the state's government back to its elected officials on December 20th, an early Christmas present for the state. However, things did not go smoothly from there. Shortly after the new year, senators for Georgia were selected and sent to Washington, where they received a hot-tempered and exclusive reception. The senators, Alexander Stephen and Herschel Johnson, were both ex-Confederates. Stephens, as you may recall, was the former vice president of the Confederacy, and Johson had been a Confederate senator. Regardless, they were chosen by the Georgia government as senators because of their popularity, tenure as statesmen, and moderation in their

---

[22] Bragg, William. "Reconstruction in Georgia." New Georgia Encyclopedia, last modified Sep 30, 2020.

views (which they were even as Confederates). The US Senate, however, did not see it this way. Neither of the Georgia senators nor anyone in the House of Representatives was permitted to take their seat in Congress.

This set a precedent for how the next few years would be.

Freed People

With 460,000 former slaves freed during and after the Civil War in Georgia, the state was facing a labor shortage it had never seen before. So much of the South's economy was built on the back of the cotton industry, which had been entirely possible because of the growing slave population. For perspective, in 1865, the cotton harvest was around 50,000 bales compared to a high in 1860 of more than 700,000 bales; that is a decline of 90 percent of the harvest from 1860 to months after the Civil War ended.[23] When harvest came in the fall of 1865, many freed men and women took to the cities rather the fields to enjoy their new lives. However, with the influx of people, many Georgian cities became quickly overcrowded. As a result, disease and food shortages were common. Due to the spread of disease, many freed people lost their lives.

About that same time, the Freedmen's Bureau became an active agent in the lives of the emancipated slaves. Officially known as the Bureau of Refugees, Freedmen, and Abandoned Lands, the US Congress created it to "aid African Americans undergoing the transition from slavery to freedom in the aftermath of the Civil War."[24] As the first welfare program to exist in the country, the Freedmen's Bureau became an active agent in the lives of Southerners. Primarily, in the fall of 1865, it focused on resettlement and land management for former slaves. By managing the land program in Georgia, the Bureau was able to act as a "middleman" that mediated contracts between former slaves and white landowners for work that earned fair pay for labor. One advantage at this time was that freedwomen, who formerly had to work the fields with their husbands, now had the choice to leave the field to settle homes and be with their children. Both children and adults were now able to seek educational opportunities provided by Northern (or formerly Northern) teachers; these opportunities often accompanied all black churches in the South.

---

[23] Bragg, William. "Reconstruction in Georgia."

[24] Hatfield, Edward. "Freedmen's Bureau." New Georgia Encyclopedia, last modified Sep 16, 2020.

While many white Georgians expected emancipation to mean something similar to what it did in the Antebellum period, there were actually some systemic changes that helped the freed people push back against the assumptions of their white neighbors. While they were still not seen as full citizens and voters, freed people earned a lot more rights in Georgia than any other former Confederate state. One example was that Georgia did not create a harsh Black Code like many other Southern states. In fact, the Georgia General Assembly afforded "practical civil equality."

> "[Freed people] had access to the courts in being able to make and enforce contracts, to sue and to be sued. They also gained property rights, which meant they could buy, sell, inherit, and lease both land and personal property. They were not to be subjected to any punishment or penalty that did not apply to whites as well. Their marriages and children were legitimized."

The Republican Party still had to fight for more rights for freed people and had a growing concern about policies they believed endangered freed people's security, such as not being able to serve on a jury, vote, or testify against whites in court.

Congressional Reconstruction

From 1867 to 1868, after a sweeping Republican victory in Congress, a new era of Reconstruction would begin. Rather than being spearheaded by the president, the newly elected Ulysses S. Grant, it would be managed by the Republican-led Congress.

With the Republican Congress in control, two new acts were pushed through: the Fourteenth Amendment and a renewal of Reconstruction. Under congressional Reconstruction, Georgia was once again not part of the Union and was placed under military occupation. Along with Florida and Alabama, Georgia made up the Third Military District under the supervision of Union General John Pope. Per congressional order, Pope worked to get all of the eligible voters in Georgia, both white and black, registered to elect another set of new delegates for a constitutional convention.

There were almost 200,000 eligible voters, and the number was split almost perfectly between white and black. According to Bragg, a Georgian historian, there was a total of 95,214 white voters registered and 93,457 black voters registered. What is particularly worthy of note is that those black voters had not recently moved to Georgia but rather represented how many black men had been living in Georgia prior to the Civil War (even with some having moved to the North during and after the war). With the passage of the Fourteenth Amendment nationwide, even if the former Confederate States were not part of ratification, those black voters were given full rights and citizenship. From here on out, their voice would dramatically shift the political powers in Georgia.

The convention and its delegates, including thirty-seven African Americans, met in Atlanta from December 1867 through March 1868. While they met, there was a drastic two-day convention held in Macon by radical Republicans where they bemoaned the Constitutional Convention, democratic policy, and black political participation,

During the course of the convection, two other big political moves occurred. In Georgia, Governor Jenkins was removed from office. After spending a significant amount of time working to stabilize the state's finances and reestablishing the state's credit lines, he was irate when General Pope drafted $40,000 from the state treasury to pay for the Constitutional Convention. His efforts to protest Pope's "illegal" withdrawal eventually ended with his removal from office by Pope's successor, General George G Meade. Meade replaced Jenkins with a new military governor, General Thomas Ruger. At that same time, January of 1868, just a few months before Ulysses S. Grant's presidential inauguration, President Johnson was impeached, given his trial in the Senate, and very nearly convicted.

As the convention progressed in spite of the political turmoil around them, the delegates successfully framed a new state constitution. A few new provisions stand out from the rest. There was a new provision for blacks to vote, a free public education system, and debt relief. Wives were given control of their personal property, governors would now serve for four years instead of two, and the state's seat of government would be moved from Milledgeville to Atlanta.

That April, a set of votes occurred. Georgia voters were asked whether or not to ratify the new state constitution and to elect state officers and US congressmen. The new constitution was ratified in a close vote. Republican candidate Rufus Bullock was elected governor over Democratic candidate John B. Gordon. In the Georgia State Assembly, eighty-four Republicans were elected to office but were in the minority, as eighty-eight Democrats were also elected. Twenty-nine of the new Republican assemblymen were black. The Georgia Senate ended up being a Republican-controlled body with twenty-seven seats to the Democrats' seventeen. - Three of the Republicans were black.

Three New Terms

After the April 1868 election, three new "groups" rose up within the political arena. While none of these groups were a legitimate voting bloc, they were labeled and widely known throughout the South, including Georgia.

The first group was known as carpetbaggers. These were any individuals who moved from the North to the South to take political office after the Civil War. These individuals were named by white conservatives and generally abhorred for this tactic. This was made possible by a Reconstruction policy that only required political nominees to live for one year in the state they were seeking election in to be eligible. Scalawags, on the other hand, were white, Southern-born Republicans whom many white conservatives felt had betrayed their heritage.

With these two terms in mind, in Georgia, the government was far more scalawag than carpetbagger. Both stateside and in Congress, Georgia did not have many carpetbaggers compared to other Southern states. Even Governor Bullock, though originally from New York, was considered a Georgian because he moved south years before the Civil War began and had served in the Confederate Army. The most well-known scalawag was former Governor Joseph Brown, who flipped to the Republican Party in 1868. John Emory Bryant, who moved down from Maine as a Freedmen's Bureau officer, was the major carpetbagger in the Georgia government.

The third and most infamous group that arose at this time was the terrorist wing of the Democratic Party: the Ku Klux Klan (KKK). In its earliest iteration, the KKK was a group of "night riders who acted to suppress Republicans of all races and origins" through whatever means necessary.[25] Some historians believe that the KKK made their debut in Georgia by killing a Republican judge and Senate candidate, George Ashburn. Black leaders from all walks of life made for more important targets than white Republicans.

---

[25] Bragg, William. "Reconstruction in Georgia."

Backslide

While the initial state government in 1868 was a raging success, it did not last for long. In its early days, the Bullock administration was able to pass the Fourteenth Amendment through the legislation, seat a Republican governor (Bullock), and be readmitted to the Union. By July, not even a full two months after inauguration, the Democratic Party in Georgia held a rally bent on expressing their contempt for all things Republican, from Joseph Brown to Ulysses Grant. It was about that time that Brown was seated on the state Supreme Court as chief justice, which had to have cheered Democrats since they no longer needed to fight him in the legislature.

By the next month, the Georgia Assembly Democrats (along with some Republican allies) began working to expel black legislators. According to Brown, they said, the constitution did not give them any right to do this. The great irony of the September expulsion of black legislators from the Georgia Assembly is that the Democrats expelled men who defended the right of ex-Confederates (who were mostly Democrats) to serve in the assembly, regardless of their past. To heighten the tensions regarding blacks in post-Reconstruction Georgia, the Camilla Massacre left twelve blacks dead and many whites wounded just before a black Republican rally in the city of Camilla.

Bullock, for his part, was also a target of the Democrats. Between the Camilla Massacre, the unseating of the black assemblymen, and Georgia being only one of two ex-Confederate states to vote for Republican Ulysses S. Grant, Bullock repeatedly called for a renewed military occupation of the state, which drew the ire of the Democrats.

For their part, Democrats regularly tried to disrupt the administration in Georgia. They regularly charged the Bullock administration with fraud, corruption, and general wrongdoing. Add to this the fact that the Republicans themselves were split on their support for Bullock (in part because of his calls for occupation), and it becomes obvious that a coalition could not be formed to affect change or progress in Georgia.

That was until June of 1869, the following summer, when the Republicans finally had some victories. In *White v. Clements*, with a deciding vote from Joseph Brown, blacks won the constitutional right in Georgia to hold public office. By January 1870, the last military governor of the Third Military District and ardent opponent of the KKK, Alfred Terry, began a "purge" of the Georgia government. He removed all former Confederates from the Georgia General Assembly and replaced them with Republicans. He went on to reinstate all of the expelled black assemblymen, which swung the majority to the Republicans. With that majority, Republicans ratified the Fifteenth Amendment and were able to reseat their senators in the US Senate.

By July 1871, Georgia was once again readmitted to the Union. It was also the last state to be readmitted.

The next ten years would be a politically tumultuous time in Georgia, which Democrats, also known as Redeemers in the early years, would control for decades. The tensions between whites and blacks would climb into the mid-1900s as racial disputes grew and economic prosperity remained out of reach for many.

Chapter 7 – Democratic Georgia and World War II

Urban Hopes and Populism

For the first eighteen years after Reconstruction, a band of former Confederates grabbed hold of power in Georgia. Known as the "Bourbon Triumvirate," Joseph Brown, John B. Gordon, and Alfred Colquitt all held positions as governor and/or senator long enough to profit handsomely from the industrialization of Georgia, which they advocated and supported. Henry Grady, the editor of the *Atlanta Constitution*, also advocated building a "prosperous 'New South' centered around [industrialized] Atlanta."[26] Like a phoenix rising from the ashes of war, as Grady would say, Atlanta was ready to be a magnetic capital of the progressive New South. Although Grady's vision ran counter to what many nationally and even state-wide thought of Atlanta, Grady did not give up for much of the 1880s.

However, even with his best efforts, Grady's vision did not come to pass. While Atlanta might have seen some growth and slow industrialization, Georgia as a whole remained predominantly rural. All across the state, farm owners and sharecroppers alike sought to survive; they did not care how dynamic, progressive, or prosperous Atlanta could become. With the loss of slave labor, as mentioned before, the farm industry took a huge hit in cotton production and began to fall into a

---

[26] Cobb, James and John Inscoe. "Georgia History."

major financial pitfall. By 1880, 45 percent of all farmers, black and white, had to begin participating in the crop lien and tenant systems; in 1920, that had risen to about 66 percent. Generational farmers, who had lived and worked their own land for decades (if not a century), were more likely than not to be working on land they did not own or sharecropping.

One result of this circumstance was the rise of the Farmers' Alliance. Once a Texas organization, by the late 1880s, it had spread to almost the entire South. In short, the Farmers' Alliance was established by white farmers to help solve the growing financial problems of Southern farms. The Farmers' Alliance would advocate for "cooperative purchasing and marketing enterprise" while also petitioning for federal farm credits.[27] From these efforts, the Farmers' Alliance effectively established a burgeoning political third party. However, when its efforts for federal credit failed, it helped other similar organizations form an official third party: the People's Party, better known as the Populist Party.

Under the unofficial leadership of Thomas E. Watson, the Populist Party created a nationally recognized platform based on banking and railroad reform alongside the other Farmers' Alliance policies. Unlike the Farmers' Alliance, which was a white-organized and white-supporting organization, the Populist Party was inclusive. It represented and encouraged black participation in the new movement. This advocacy is what drove many to oppose and clash with the new party ahead of its demise after the McKinley election, in which would-be President William McKinley borrowed Populist ideas to win the election for the Republicans.

Jim Crow

With the fall of the Populist movement, Georgia (or rather, colored Georgians) had to suffer under two new efforts to subvert what little power they had gained over the last three decades: Jim Crow and a resurgence of the KKK.

In the 1890s, most Southern states began the process of passing laws to ensure racial segregation and essentially codify white superiority. You may have heard of things like "separate but equal" facilities, such as water fountains, public restrooms, and schools. These laws grew to become known as Jim Crow laws, though no one is sure why the old character from the 1920s and 1930s was adopted for these laws. Besides "separate

---

[27] Hild, Matthew. "Farmers' Alliance." New Georgia Encyclopedia, last modified May 16, 2016.

but equal" facilities, colored voters were disenfranchised at the polls, discriminated against in housing and for employment, and were often refused public accommodations. Most of the Jim Crow laws remained until the 1960s.

Three notable conditions contributed to the hastening of Jim Crow laws in the 1890s after years of white and black relations that were not only tenable but also thriving:

1. The growing trust in the idea of "scientific racism"
2. The overseas subjugation of non-whites in the Philippines, Hawaii, and Cuba (after the Spanish-American War)
3. White response to black calls for an expansion of civil rights.[28]

Hatfield, an expert on the Georgia civil rights movement, stated that "efforts undertaken by Black petitioners in the late nineteenth century sometimes hastened Jim Crow's rise. When confronted with Black demands for an expansion of civil rights, whites often responded by calling for a more comprehensive legal code to bar racial interaction altogether."[29] At first glance, it could be seen that Hatfield is making the case that black communities who self-advocated were at fault for their own, though eventual, suffering under Jim Crow laws. However, it must be understood that under the Constitution leading up to Jim Crow, African Americans had rather vague rights as citizens. Their advocacy came from a place of trying to clarify and codify their place in society, but that was met with a desire to codify laws of suppression. Eventually, that suppression would become the status quo in culture, and any pushback was an assault on the American lifestyle and culture itself. This is why the civil rights movement was sometimes violent.

In each case, either the culture of the day or the laws of the land ingrained racism into the people. Now, we must admit that these three conditions are not comprehensive or adequate enough to explain all of the nuances of growing racism and segregation in the South and Georgia. However, they can help us to have a set of lenses by which we can observe the events of the 1890s to 1960s to see how things slowly declined and how tensions grew leading up to the civil rights movement.

---

[28] Hatfield. "Segregation."

[29] Hatfield. "Segregation."

Since the poll taxes of the 1870s had been deemed illegal, the ruling party had to find creative ways to keep blacks, who were typically Republican, from participating. Their final solution included amending the state constitution in 1908 to require voters to pass a literacy test and meet property requirements. As a result, both blacks and many poor whites were barred from the polls. By disenfranchising poor whites, the ruling class was able to make the state more attractive to investors by removing some of the more radical elements from their ranks.

When the Supreme Court ruled in the case of *Plessy v. Ferguson*, a case about segregation in Louisiana, it granted official sanctions to the "separate but equal" laws all across the South, opening the doors for those laws to go beyond facilities to include restaurants, theaters, neighborhoods, and all schools. "Equal" was in name only, as many colored facilities were rundown, underserviced, and clearly inferior to white facilities. For example, on average, Georgia spent $43 per white student in 1930 but only $10 per black student in the public school system.

While there were advocates in the colored communities who tried to end Jim Crow laws, there were louder and more incendiary voices in the white community who sought to inflame the tensions between the two groups. Newspapers were often the most incendiary, printing stories of black crime (which might or might not have been completely accurate) and not caring about the consequences. More often than not, the consequences were violence against colored members of that community, even those who had not committed a crime.

There are three prime examples to help you see how the violence got worse over time. First, there was the Atlanta Race Massacre. In the aftermath of a newspaper publication about black-on-white rape, white mobs spent three days (September 24th to 26th, 1906) killings black men in Atlanta. When it was all done, dozens had been killed, more wounded, and extensive property damage had been committed.

The second-best example was the lynchings that occurred throughout the state. From 1882 to 1930, many whites resorted to lynchings to "maintain the ... racial caste system" of the time.[30] In that time period, Georgia had the second-highest number of lynchings of any Southern state, with a total of 458 mob killings by hanging, burning, drowning, dismemberment, shooting, or by dragging the black victim behind a horse

---

[30] Hatfield. "Segregation."

at high speeds until death. Only Mississippi had more, with 538 deaths. Some historians would indicate that the real number of victims in Georgia numbered over 3,000, but only 458 were documented.[31]

Our last example involves the KKK. In 1916, the Ku Klux Klan had a resurgence at Stone Mountain. This revived KKK was both a threat to black and Jewish communities, especially after the lynching of Leo Frank, a Jew accused of murder, in 1915. While the violence of the "new Klan" might not have been what it was immediately after the Civil War, it got worse over time, with attacks on property and African Americans as the civil rights movement got closer. This time around, they widely appealed to successful businessmen or other middle-class workers, making them a powerful political influence against the groups they opposed.

Jim Crow laws and all the evil that entailed continued for many years. While it was opposed by some, it was not toppled for many years. While we may never be able to fully understand or comprehend the circumstances the black communities of that time endured, we can still attempt to picture life from their perspective.

Author Lillian Smith, a Georgian, paints a rather honest and heartbreaking image of the Jim Crow period from the African American perspective in her memoir *Killers of the Dream*:

> "From the time little southern children take their first step they learn their ritual, for Southern Tradition leads them through its intricate movements. And some, if their faces are dark, learn to bend, hat in hand; and some, if their faces are white, learn to hold their heads up high. Some step off the sidewalk while others pass by in arrogance. Bending, shoving, genuflecting, ignoring, stepping off, demanding, giving in, avoiding...So we learned the dance that cripples the human spirit, step by step by step, we who were white and we who were colored, day by day, hour by hour, year by year until the movements were reflexes and made for the rest of our lives without thinking."

The Great Depression and World War II

Before the onset of the Great Depression in the United States, Georgia was suffering its own crisis. Where the Dust Bowl would eventually cause

---

[31] Tolnay, Stewart and E. Beck. "Lynching." New Georgia Encyclopedia, last modified Aug 12, 2020.

agricultural harm in the Midwest, the boll weevil and migration did the same in Georgia. After the invasive boll weevil was introduced into the state, there was a 75 percent drop in production between 1918 and 1923. To compound the issue, about 400,000 Georgia residents migrated to other parts of the country in the 1920s, many of whom were black; this migration contributed to the 50 percent drop in agricultural workers between 1910 and 1930 as the Great Depression was settling in.

However, as significant as these negative events were, the New Deal was equally as transformative for Georgia agriculture. President Franklin D. Roosevelt, who was elected at the beginning of the Depression, quickly went into action to raise the prices of agricultural goods, though it required a reduction in production to increase demand. FDR's Agricultural Adjustment Administration, a program he began in his first one hundred days, oversaw this reduction. As a result, you may assume, many farmers were now out of work and seeking other jobs. To fill the unemployment gap, many small, low-wage businesses moved into some of Georgia's small, formerly agricultural towns.

Now, you may be thinking, why did the Georgian farmers let the president enact a policy that put them out of work? In short, they were actually rather friendly with the president and were familiar with the man from New York.

After contracting a case of polio in 1921, Roosevelt (known more often as FDR) visited Warm Springs, Georgia, to rest in the waters there and try to rehabilitate his legs. These visits began in 1924 and continued until his untimely death in 1945, which occurred in Warm Springs. FDR "quickly grew to love Georgia and its people, and they welcomed him as their adopted son."[32] While resting in Georgia each spring and fall, FDR would often go for drives or train rides across the countryside of Georgia. It is suspected that on these drives, where he met farmers and other agricultural workers, he developed plans, such as the Agricultural Adjustment Administration and others. Some, we can imagine, were created in his mind well before his election to president.

With all that in mind, it is not surprising that during the 1932 presidential election, Georgia gave strong and excited support from day

---

[32] Minchew, Kaye. "Franklin D. Roosevelt in Georgia." New Georgia Encyclopedia, last modified Aug 14, 2020. https://www.georgiaencyclopedia.org/articles/history-archaeology/franklin-d-roosevelt-in-georgia/.

one. Throughout FDR's presidency, he leveraged time in Georgia to gain political capital with the state while also working to improve the people's lives. His wife, Eleanor, was also well known in Georgia as an advocate for desegregation and civil rights, though FDR did not press these issues for fear of political backlash. Over his almost twelve years in office, he still visited Warm Springs, where he died of a stroke in 1945.

While many farmers had been out of work throughout the 1930s, and what jobs they could get required they labor for little pay, there was a light at the end of the tunnel.

As the 1930s and 1940s moved forward, two industries grew in Georgia. First was Georgia's aviation industry, which would really boom in the 1940s. In 1923, the would-be mayor of Atlanta, William B Hartsfield, established an airport in the city that would later become Atlanta International Airport. Within two decades, the airport served as a "major hub for both Eastern Air Lines and Delta Air Lines."[33] Second, with the nation's entry into World War II, industry across the nation boomed like never before, creating numerous new jobs across the country. The Georgia economy boomed as a result of a few things, specifically the following:

- Soldiers came to Fort Bennings for training. At the time, it was the largest training facility for infantrymen in the whole world.
- Bell Aircraft Corporation, known then as Bell Bomber, produced B-29 airplanes in Marietta, Georgia, from 1943 until the war ended. They employed over twenty-eight thousand workers.
- With its fifteen thousand workers, the Southeastern Shipbuilding Corp produced over two hundred "Liberty Ships" in the ports of Brunswick and Savannah.

The effects of these and other industrial efforts cannot be overstated enough. The average annual income increased by over 100 percent in ten years, from $350 to $1,000 before 1950 in Georgia (this was well above the national average). Georgia was able to hold on to this industrial growth coming out of the war, and Atlanta remained a transportation hub.

---

[33] Cobb, James and John Inscoe. "Georgia History."

Chapter 8 – Civil Rights Era

While the headlines for this era come primarily from the 1950s and 1960s, there was a lot of work, tears, and blood that went into Georgia civil rights long before then. Resistance to segregation and race-based lifestyle choices began all the way back in the earlier years of the 20th century. Often, in the early years, civil rights reform was led by African Methodist Episcopal Church leaders like Henry Turner until organizations, such as the National Association for the Advancement of Colored People (NAACP), formed. The benefit of such organizations was that they could do a little more than just one person could, even though all across the state, individuals and families were responsible for establishing schools, churches, and other social organizations within segregated communities.

World War II Era Protests

With the growth of urban living and the uptick of economic development during and after World War Two, along with the benefits of the New Deal, the "planter elite" began to decline in power. Farmers and landowners were no longer the power brokers in Georgia; instead, those who lived in the cities gained more power. Paired with the opportunities to serve in the military during the war, blacks were finally able to see and seize an opportunity to push back against white supremacy. The war and its fight for European democracy set the stage for a chance to press for true democracy stateside as well, and the African American leaders at the time led the charge for racial change in the South.

One of the first attempts at reformation began with the legal challenge of *King v. Chapman et al.* In this case, a man named Primus King was recruited by activist Dr. Thomas Brewer to attempt to vote in the Georgia Democratic primary in 1944. Both men knew King would be turned away at the ballot box, and they were right. A year later, they sued and won the case. The decision was upheld again in 1946, resulting in 125,000 new black voter registrations. This allowed black leaders all across the state, but especially in cities, to elect more moderate candidates to all levels of government. As a result, these same leaders could lobby for the "Black police and higher spending for Black schools."[34] The NAACP also grew at this time to have fifty new branches.

One particular election that would affect change for African Americans was the fourth governor race of Eugene Talmadge. An unapologetic white supremacist (famous for saying that race was a "question of white supremacy"), Talmadge would willfully have undone much of the work happening for civil rights in Georgia.[35] Though he won the election of 1946, he died before taking office, which was given to his son, Henry, in a scandal known as the three governors controversy. Unfortunately, Talmadge was able to highlight the flaws of the Georgia system by winning through some degree of fraud, violence, and the abuse of the county unit election system.[36] He and his supporters were able to systematically disqualify many black voters from the rolls. Though not as experienced as his father, Henry Talmadge was still responsible for a revival of white supremacy in Georgia. The revival had the Georgia civil rights movement backpedaling: segregation was doubled down, the NAACP fell under attack from state officials (so badly that its leader resigned), and white supremacy vigilantes targeted and killed black community leaders. Dr. Brewer was one of the assassinations that took place during the late 1940s and early 1950s. One political attack that was made on the civil rights movement was the supremacists' choice to connect their attacks with the general fear of communism felt across the country. By accusing black leaders of being communists, they lost what little credibility they might have held in political or non-black spaces.

---

[34] Tuck, Stephen. "Civil Rights Movement." New Georgia Encyclopedia, last modified Aug 24, 2020.

[35] Tuck, Stephen. "Civil Rights Movement."

[36] The county election system was similar to the national electoral college system used in presidential races. Both allotted power to smaller units, meaning someone (like Talmadge) could lose the popular vote in the state but still win the election.

Even in the midst of the Talmadge years, two victories came for the black community. First, Atlanta, Macon, and Savannah (the three largest cities at the time) became havens for more moderate race relations. There, the protests continued and gained some traction, although it cannot go without saying that strict segregation and violence continued even in those cities. Second, the court case *Brown v. Board of Education* in Topeka, Kansas, paved the way for desegregated schools in 1954. While many whites resisted any kind of integration in schools (some even advocated for closing schools before integrating their children in them), the matter went forward, and integration decisions were made at the local level as per the Sibley Commission.

While it may seem like the Sibley Commission did a good thing here, it must be said that the committee members had to really toe the line and appease white voters. While they might have "succeeded" in keeping public schools open and began the process of integration, they also provided school boards with tactics they could use to slow down the process on the local level. As a result, many schools in Georgia were not even beginning integration until the late 1960s.

1960s Civil Rights in Georgia

Nonviolent protest became the norm in major Georgia cities beginning in the 1960s to combat segregation and white supremacy across the state. Nonviolent protests took root in Georgia because of the success they had had elsewhere in the South in the prior years. While the protests were commonplace from city to city, each of the three major urban centers had a distinct story, much like Georgia itself. Across all three, students were at the forefront of the movement.

Atlanta, being the largest and most influential, adopted the nonviolent movement the earliest. Led by two students, Lonnie King and Herschelle Sullivan, the protests in Atlanta were organized to be "sophisticated and durable;" they were meant to last and challenge the minds of their oppressors.[37] While it might have been the first city to adopt the need for protest, Atlanta was one of the last to see segregation come to an end. Without the support of more traditionally affirmed black leadership, paired with the city's carefully crafted "Too Busy to Hate" slogan, the movement could not gather the needed power to affect change. At least 103 other Southern cities beat Atlanta to the desegregation of lunch

---

[37] Tuck, Stephen. "Civil Rights Movement."

counters. By 1963, King, Herschelle, and others were even writing to the mayor of Atlanta, bemoaning how long it was taking for real change to come.

Savannah, in contrast to Atlanta, saw some changes, even if they also took years after launching a campaign in 1960. Led by NAACP head W. W. Law, the Savannah protests were "united, widespread, and unremitting" until city leaders were all but forced to agree to the terms of desegregation for public and private facilities. The protestors had their victory on October 1st, 1963, about eight months ahead of any federal legislation on the subject. Over the course of their protests, Law was fired from his job as a mail carrier but reinstated after October 1st when his court case on the matter began to look like it would become a nationwide scandal. Savannah's success was also seen in other cities like Brunswick, Macon, and Rome. Martin Luther King Jr. was quoted as describing Savannah as "the most desegregated city south of the Mason-Dixon line."[38]

King himself was actually part of a nonviolent protest in the Georgia city of Albany, where his involvement got the city's movement national headlines. King's participation in the Albany protests lasted from the fall of 1961 until the summer of 1962 and is often referred to as the Albany Movement. Unfortunately, the Albany Movement is often seen as the largest setback to King's efforts in the South; it was opposed very readily by the chief of police, made several tactical mistakes, and held divisive leadership because some student leaders felt King's presence was causing things to go backward. While King was able to ensure more people were involved, with about one thousand protestors being jailed while he was in town, his departure did bring the Albany protests back into the hands of volunteers and students who would eventually have more success in the city.

Two other large cities faced struggles of their own. In Augusta, violence was used to oppose many of the protesters. Meanwhile, in Columbus, protests were rarely seen because the African American community was still processing the murder of Thomas Brewer; who would want to protest after that level of violence?

While the cities were hubs for protestors, they were not alone in the fight. Many rural communities had their own brand of protests, and none of them were going well. The roots of white supremacy ran so deep in

---

[38] Tuck, Stephen. "Civil Rights Movement."

rural Georgia that it was often quipped that the civil rights movement ended south of Atlanta. Keep in mind, too, that rural Georgia was still struggling economically many years after Reconstruction since most of the population had moved to urban centers. This, in a sad and painful twist of fate, all but required rural African Americans to rely on their white counterparts.

However, it cannot be understated that the violence in rural areas against protestors was far worse than that of cities, and this effectively tamped down some rural efforts. In counties such as Terrell and Baker, located in the southwest portion of the state, even the police grew violent. The Student Nonviolent Coordinating Committee (SNCC) had some members move to these areas to "battle for the minds" of the formerly enslaved in addition to their mission to register black voters.[39] It will not surprise you that many of these students died; many were shot, but others were charged with insurrection and expected execution for their "crimes" before they were eventually released. Knowing it would take years, if not a generation, many of the students made these counties their permanent home as they worked to win the battle.

When two pieces of federal legislation were passed, many thought the fight for civil rights was won and that things would change for the better.

They were mostly right, but they were also horribly wrong.

In 1963, President John F. Kennedy sent a civil rights bill to Congress, where it was bogged down in committee by a Mississippi senator who ardently supported segregation. With the assassination of the president in November of that same year, it was up to newly inaugurated President Lyndon B. Johnson to do his best to honor the efforts made by Kennedy to advance the rights of colored Americans. And he did.

By 1964, Johnson was able to get the Civil Rights Act through Congress. The provisions of the bill were the most comprehensive and effective civil rights legislation to ever get passed by both chambers of Congress. The new law "contained provisions barring discrimination and segregation in education, public facilities, jobs, and housing" and created the Equal Employment Opportunity Commission (EEOC).[40] Not only would colored Americans be able to work in the same offices as whites,

---

[39] Tuck, Stephen. "Civil Rights Movement."

[40] Getchell, Michelle. "The Civil Rights Act of 1964 and the Voting Rights Act of 1965 (Article)." Khan Academy. Accessed September 7, 2023.

but they could also apply for and earn the same jobs as whites. The EEOC went as far as to ensure fair hiring by employers and serve local communities by supporting them in addressing or navigating civil rights issues as they popped up. The Civil Rights Act was supported by almost 75 percent of the Senate.

Not a full year later, Johnson was also able to get the Voting Rights Act of 1965 passed into law about six months after the "Bloody Sunday" attack done on six hundred activists on a march from Selma to Montgomery, Alabama. The events of that March, seen on TV and in newspapers across the entire country, galvanized Johnson to defend voting rights for the disenfranchised colored communities. Passed on August 6th, 1965, the Voting Rights Act clearly "outlawed poll taxes, literacy tests, and other practices that had effectively prevented southern blacks from voting."[41] As a result, over half a million new Southern blacks registered to vote; as you can imagine, this dramatically changed the political landscape of the South.

(**A quick side note:** With so many new voters registered as a result of efforts made by the Democratic Party's leaders like President Johnson, many black voters gave their allegiance to the Democratic Party in the next several election cycles. Clearly, there had already been some changes within the platform for it to have gone from the party of Jim Crow in the early 1900s to the advocate of desegregation, but after the Voting Rights Act, many white segregationists (now disenchanted with the party) swung to the Republican Party. This swing, along with the campaign run by presidential hopeful Richard Nixon in the 1970s to win over Southerners to the Republican Party, are the final events that give us the Republican and Democratic Parties we are familiar with today.)

In the following years, President Johnson named the first black Cabinet member, Robert C. Weaver, who became the housing and urban development secretary, and appointed Thurgood Marshall as the first African American justice on the United States Supreme Court.

Unfortunately, even with so many achievements at the federal level, Georgia was still, in many ways, left in the dust of what should have been a momentous victory. Interestingly, while the South had earned half a million new voters after the Voting Rights Act of 1965, as late as 1980, Georgia had African Americans holding less than one-tenth of its elected

---

[41] Getchell, Michelle. "The Civil Rights Act of 1964 and the Voting Rights Act of 1965 (Article)."

offices. Although the civil rights legislation addressed rights and voting, it did little, if nothing, to address the circumstances many poorer blacks faced in Georgia. They faced problems of unemployment, dilapidated housing, and police brutality. What good was the right to vote when the local police could still beat you on your walk home from work at night?

These sorts of issues spurred the summer riots of 1965. The worst riot in the state occurred later in 1970 when a black teenager was tortured and murdered inside the Augusta city jail. While his murder might have triggered the riot, years of tension are known to be the real cause.

However, the African American community was not the only one to publicly decry the results of federal legislation. In many rural counties, white Georgians protested the integration of schools. This protest would carry on in some places for years, even after the "forced integration" was over and done. In those same communities, though, poor blacks and whites would struggle for years to overcome the economic hardship that had shaped their lives for decades.

While it is easy to cast a cynical or dour eye on history, it must be said that the efforts made by activists, mothers, students, employees, and government leaders to empower the African American communities *did* bring about change. Their work made the lives of those who came after them better, even if they did not get to see that happen. Georgia was and still is not a perfect place, but it is still fueled by people who wish to see changes made for the better.

One Georgian would seek to do that for the whole nation.

His name?

Jimmy Carter.

Chapter 9 – Carter Years

Even after the passage of the civil rights legislation, Georgia remained a solidly Republican state. It backed every Republican nominee for president until a native Georgian and former governor, James Earl Carter Jr., ran in 1976.

Early Years

Born in Plains, Georgia, on October 1st, 1924, "Jimmy," as he liked to be called, was part of a Democratic family of farmers and small-town merchants. When he was old enough, Carter enrolled at Georgia Southwestern State University, not too far from his hometown, and would later go to Georgia Institute of Technology before being appointed to the United States Naval Academy. By 1946, he had graduated and been commissioned as a senior officer in the Navy as a member of the *Seawolf* crew, which was the second nuclear submarine to ever be built.

Carter and his wife, would-be First Lady Rosalynn (Smith) Carter, married shortly after his graduation. They had four children together: three sons and one daughter. When Carter's father, James E. Carter Sr., passed away in 1953, Jimmy Carter chose to resign his US Navy commission and the promising career that would have certainly come with it. He traded a seat on a sub for one on a tractor, working hard to restore his family's peanut farm and warehouse businesses. He wanted to look after all his father had built.

Beginnings

Business under the younger Carters was a booming success, and with Jimmy's newfound free time away from the Navy, he began to dabble in community affairs. In the years after returning to Plains, Carter held a variety of positions that Fink, a Carter biographer, highlights:

> "He served on Sumter County's library and school boards and on its hospital authority. He held leadership roles in regional and state planning associations and eventually became president of the Georgia Planning Association. He also served as state president of the Certified Seed Organization and as district governor of Lions International."[42]

By 1962, Carter had secured the next step in his foray into governing. With everything for his business squared away, Carter sought to follow his late father's steps and run for state office. His father was a representative in the state legislature, and Jimmy Carter won an unfair race to secure a seat in the state Senate. During his two terms in office, Carter would be named chair of the Senate Education Committee, which he would use to finish things he had started on the county education board. Carter had always been an ardent supporter of public education, even if some of his school mergers and efficiency programs earlier in his career were voted down because they were seen as a precursor to desegregation. In the state Senate, he would continue to advocate for a similar policy but this time with a louder voice and a farther reach.

With his second state Senate term coming to an end, Carter decided to run in the gubernatorial (governor) race. The context of the governor's race in 1966 is rather complex, with a legitimate Republican contender for the first time in a few election cycles, Democrats with all different policies going head to head, and a run-off because of write-ins. In the end, the Democrats took the seat, but it was not Carter who took the lead. He lost to both of the other Democratic nominees in the primary, one of whom, Lester Maddox, was appointed by the General Assembly because no candidate had a majority. Maddox made for an excellent foil to Cater. He had no political experience before his election, ran several restaurants in the city, and was a staunch segregationist who opposed the notion of civil rights. Maddox was known for having black activists and nonviolent protesters forcefully removed from his restaurant during sit-ins at lunch

---

[42] Fink, Gary. "Jimmy Carter." New Georgia Encyclopedia, last modified Nov 3, 2020.

counters.

Although Carter lost, he was ready to run again. In his second gubernatorial campaign, Carter took the "good ole boy" route, projecting himself as an everyman's man and a traditional Southern conservative. His appeals won the day, and Carter took the office of governor of Georgia in 1970. In a speech that shocked the nation and earned its attention, Carter declared that "No poor, rural, weak, or Black person should ever have to bear the additional burden of being deprived of the opportunity of an education, a job, or simple justice."[43]

In one breath, Carter unveiled his true hopes: to lead government reforms in Georgia that fit a moderate business progressive view. Just like in his family business and the state school system, Jimmy Carter sought to make the state government more efficient and able to meet the needs of all its citizens.

Reform and efficiency were the rule of law for the Georgia executive branch under Carter. It may have taken most of his four-year term, but Carter was able to accomplish an astonishing amount. Carter was able to take the state's sixty-five budgeted agencies and commissions and consolidate them into three super agencies: the Departments of Human Resources, Administrative Services, and Natural Resources. In doing so, Carter eliminated redundancies, improved the delivery of services, and reduced the state budget. He was also able to take two hundred unbudgeted agencies and reduce them into a twenty-line list of agencies, boards, bureaus, and commissions.

On top of Carter's organizational and budgeting reforms, he continued to be an advocate for the state education system. His state education reform package was called the Adequate Program for Education in Georgia. Carter's plan, which was almost entirely accomplished by the time his term was up, "provided funds to support vocational education, reduce class size, and equalize funding among districts ... increased the state's commitment to preschool education and launched a campaign that eventually led to the adoption of a statewide kindergarten program."[44]

Under his governorship, others in the state government sought to reform the state criminal justice system. Of the reforms accomplished,

---

[43] Fink, Gary. "Jimmy Carter."
[44] Fink, Gary. "Jimmy Carter."

most of them centered around the unification of the state court system, standards for judicial conduct, and a new system for the selection of judges. Tangentially, Carter began new programs to address mental health, advocate civil rights, and other programs or legislation that promoted the equality of women and minorities. Carter had higher diversity in his appointments to agencies, state boards, the judiciary, and his own staff than all those who had come before him in Georgia.

POTUS

Under Georgia law at the time, after Carter's term was up, he did not run for reelection the following year. While higher office was certainly a consideration of Carter's by 1974, he found himself working for the Democratic National Committee (DNC) the summer after his time in the governor's mansion was over. In this new position, Carter oversaw midterm elections to elect Democratic senators, governors, and congressmen. It also exposed him to leaders, consultants, and donors from all across the country.

(**A quick side note:** For context, exposure within the DNC has always been a big plus for lesser-known party members, even in the age of the internet and social media. Working with or near the Democratic National Committee can launch a potential career. One example is former President Barack Obama, who was asked by the DNC to give a speech at their national convention in 2004. At the time, he was only a one-term senator, but his speech, which was given to the biggest names in Democratic politics, paved the way for him to be elected president only four years later. So, Jimmy Carter working for the DNC, even as a one-term governor in the South, was a big deal.)

When paired with the painful and demoralizing Watergate scandal plaguing the Nixon administration at the time, Carter's time with the DNC made his bid to run as a Democratic nominee in the 1976 election a no-brainer. Along with his fiscal, organizational, and progressive resume in Georgia, Carter was the prevailing victor in his party and, in a close match with incumbent President Gerald Ford, in the country at large. Once in office, Carter employed his "good 'ole boy" populism while emphasizing ethical behavior, high moral standards, and democratic principles—things former President Nixon had flubbed on. A casual dresser, Carter's Georgia charm worked to reduce the pomp that had often been associated with the presidency. His predecessor, Gerald Ford, had some small part to do with that as well, as he landed in the midst of the mess created after

Watergate.

Leaning into his Georgia governing roots, Carter created two new Cabinet positions in the executive branch: energy and education. Neither should be surprising given how he reorganized the Georgia government to have an executive department devoted to natural resources and his devotion to improving public education. Carter also appointed a record-breaking number of minorities and women to federal positions.

During his time in office, Carter ran up against many challenges. OPEC caused intentional oil shortages, raising prices for gas and other goods in the United States. Interest rates rose, and unemployment was stagnant. Iran and the Soviet Union frustrated and embarrassed the Carter administration abroad. Many would critique Carter's choices and deem the one-term president a relative failure, but he did have many successes:

- Conservation lands, wildlife refuges, and national parks were all added in Alaska
- The Camp David Accords between Israel and Egypt were written and signed.
- Diplomatic channels were opened with China.
- An arms limitation treaty was signed with the Soviet Union.
- Carter managed both the Afghanistan invasion and the Tehran embassy seizure judiciously.
- Panama Canal treaties were negotiated.

Much of what Carter accomplished in his four-year term helped to set the stage for much of the international success of his successor, a charismatic California governor named Ronald Reagan.

Life after the White House

After his loss in the 1980 presidential election, Carter and his family returned to Georgia, where he and his wife founded the Carter Center in Atlanta. The Carter Center exists as a non-partisan organization that seeks to "Wage Peace, Fight Disease, Build Hope."[45] In the early days, the Carter Center would analyze and make recommendations about international and domestic policies while working to advocate for human rights, promote democracy, and help end conflicts peaceably.

Through his own personal efforts and those done through the 2000 programs at the Carter Center, Jimmy Carter was awarded the Nobel

---

[45] Carter Center Mission Statement.

Peace Prize in 2002 for his advocacy for peaceful resolutions on the international stage and his advancement of human rights around the world. While many negative things can be said of his time in the Oval Office, Georgia's native son was able to use that as a leaping pad to bring change around the world for over forty years.

In the intervening years, he has been an author, novelist, poet, advocate, traveler, healer, and hope dispenser. None of it would have been possible, though, were it not for a little peanut farm in Plains, Georgia.

Chapter 10 – Modern Georgia

Since the Carter years, Georgia has experienced growth and vitality mixed in with what many other Southern states have endured: loss of family-owned enterprises to larger corporate hosts.

The 20th Century

The Atlanta metro area grew steadily in the last few decades of the 20th century. As it grew, so did its prominence on the national stage. Over the years, several large companies found a home in Atlanta. United Parcel Services (UPS) is headquartered in the city alongside three Georgia-grown companies: Coca-Cola, the Home Depot, and CNN's mother company, Turner Broadcasting. These Georgia originals, as you are probably well aware, have thrived beyond the state's borders.

Atlanta was also given the world's attention when it played host to the 1996 Summer Olympic Games. This opportunity was not only a great way to earn publicity on a global scale for Georgia, but it also allowed the city of Atlanta to build some long-standing infrastructure improvements and the venues needed for the Olympic Games, some of which are still open to the public.

People who attended the 1996 Summer Olympics also witnessed a domestic terrorist attack. A man named Eric Rudolph created a pipe bomb, with the blast killing one person and injuring over one hundred others.

The Peach State retained its reputation during this time, as its peach production, along with peanuts and onions, remained high in the southern counties like where President Carter was raised. Unfortunately, farming declined rapidly. From 1950 to 2000, the number of farms in Georgia dropped from around one million to a mere sixty-three thousand. The most common cause for the farming drop-off was the decline in occupational desire and many family-run farms being bought up by larger operations.

The 21st Century

Rural Georgia did not just take a hit to its farming industry over the last four decades; its manufacturing was also impacted. Some estimate that about ninety-eight thousand jobs have been lost to overseas transition, most of which were centered on textiles and apparel. Ironically, this was the industry that helped to drive the vicious cycles of slavery, cotton production, and exports to the North prior to the Civil War.

In all honesty, since the turn of the century, Georgia has been hit again and again with troubles. After the loss of those manufacturing jobs, there was an influx of immigration that helped to prop up the construction and service sectors. However, after the economic recession of 2008, many of those same workers left the industries they had joined. Not only that, but the state also had to adjust and cut its budget at around the same time. One of the most affected budget lines was public education—a cut we can all guess hurt the heart of the former president.

Even with all of these hardships, Georgia has continued to grow. Atlanta has become one of the ten largest metropolitan areas in the country, passing Boston and Detroit. The city is home to twenty-eight counties. New industries continue to move to Georgia, like car manufacturing from Kia Motors and sections of the film industry (Marvel, Disney, and others have had shoots in Georgia in the last ten years, most of them multiple times). With all the changes and growth, tourism has become a large portion of the state's GDP (gross domestic product).

Politically, Georgia has been a swing state in several presidential elections since 2008, when President Obama won a resounding majority of the African American vote but still lost the state. After years of being a Democratic state, it had its first Republican governor since Reconstruction in 2003 when Sonny Perdue won the gubernatorial race. Since then, particularly since 2018, there has been a slow shift back toward Democratic politics, which is likely due, in large part, to the growing size and growing influence of the Atlanta metro area.

Conclusion

For what it lacks in size and influence, Georgia makes up for in its history.

It is without a doubt that the United States of America, if not the entire world, would be vastly different were it not for Georgia.

What if... Spain successfully invaded from Spanish Florida? The Carolinas and all their cash crops would have been easy pickings for Spain.

What if... Geroge Whitefield did not follow his calling to the New World to join the Wesley brothers in Georgia? America would not have had a great unifying voice willing to ride hundreds of miles on horseback. Would the colonies have stood a chance in the Revolutionary War without that unity?

What if... Eli Whitney did not have a place to travel and tutor? Would he have seen the fields and the hard work done by the slaves? We can imagine that if he had not invented the cotton gin, the need for slave labor would have certainly died out eventually and perhaps even averted the Civil War.

You get the point. Georgia was home to some of the most influential (or avoidable) moments in American history. But the amazing thing about Georgia's history is that it has affected more than just its own nation; it has also impacted those around the world. Let's look at one more scenario.

What if... Jimmy Carter's family didn't have a peanut farm in southwest Georgia that needed managing after his father passed? What if the man who negotiated peace in parts of the Middle East, who had Americans freed from an embassy assault, who helped to reopen communication with China, and who began a globally engaging non-profit that seeks peace, advocacy, and equality never went "home" and saw the need to serve on Sumter County's library and school boards?

History is amazing because we get the chance to explore the what-ifs of life as we know it. Granted, it would be great to have seen some more positive what-ifs come true during Jim Crow, but now we must reckon with the past and strive toward a better future. Without history, we can have no stories to tell the next generation to inspire them to work hard like **LBJ** or sacrifice like **Thomas Brewer** to make the world a more equitable place.

The Peach State is far more than just fruit, films, and reform; it is the story of all of us, a story riddled with setbacks, challenges, and victories. It is easy to think of Georgia as just "another" state with a similar story to the other forty-nine or, at least, the other twelve originals. But the state of Georgia is unique.

The status quo has been tested and will be tested again and again in Georgia. If history has shown us anything, it is that things certainly do not stay the same forever.

Part 2: The Cherokees

A Captivating Guide to the History of a Native American Tribe, the Cherokee Removal, and the Trail of Tears

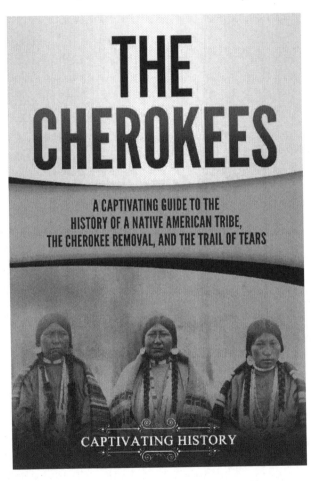

Introduction

Have you ever wondered how we came to be? How the sun came to rise in the morning and set in the evenings? Or perhaps why and how diseases came to plague humanity? There are reasons for everything, whether it be gravity, bacteria and viruses, or chemical combustion. There are reasons, but then there are answers.

The Cherokee have the answers. The Sun hates the people on Earth because when humans look at her, all they do is squint. On the other hand, the Moon loves the people because they smile and gaze upon the night's shining beauty. These are the answers, the tales that have spun across generations. They have survived disease, genocide, war, and poverty. Despite the colonizers' greatest efforts, these stories survived and are still passed on today.

The Cherokee existed on this land long before the settlers arrived. Close to twenty-three thousand years ago, what would become the Cherokee Nation crossed the Bering Land Bridge. This span of earth ran from northeastern Asia to Alaska. After the people arrived, they slowly migrated south.

The Cherokees' history began long before Columbus set sail and long before the English settlers arrived on Roanoke. But history didn't record it. Western history relies on the written word, and the Cherokee did not develop a syllabary—similar to an alphabet—until the 1800s. Instead, their history was passed down orally. Oral tradition is still kept alive in the stories shared at campfires, powwows, or the kitchen table. This cultural practice is one of the many things that sets the Cherokee and the other

Indigenous peoples of America apart from the rest.

American history tends to begin and end with the written word. Without written documents or stories, history is erased and forgotten, leaving many people behind with it. As is often heard and said, history is written by the victors. Two keywords here: written and victors.

When we look at Indigenous history, it's clear who was writing it from the 1600s onward. Without alphabets or syllabaries, many Native American tribes relied solely on oral tales to keep track of their history. So, US history was initially written by the colonizers, not by the first inhabitants of the land.

Let's consider the word victor. Who is the victor in American history? Or in the constant struggle between Native American independence and the settlers' wish for liberty and the American dream? In many ways, the colonizers were victorious. They got their wish, but in the process, they pillaged and plundered the land, ridding it of the majority of its native inhabitants, plant life, and culture. They pushed Indigenous peoples out of their tribal lands, killed them with foreign diseases, introduced stronger alcohol into their society, and continually disrespected their culture and cultural practices.

However, even though the colonizers managed to push the Native Americans out and capture the land, they still failed in one aspect. Their culture remains. Recent resurgences can be seen online through social media. TikTok, Instagram, Facebook, and Twitter have all allowed Native Americans to share their experiences with the rest of the world, highlighting the injustices they underwent years ago and today. By using the power of mass communication, young Native Americans and Indigenous peoples are dispelling the truth of the blood quantum, illuminating life on the reservation, and embracing sacred cultural practices that were once forbidden by the federal government.

This moment in history represents a huge transition. The United States is beginning to make reparations, slowly but steadily, for the atrocities that were committed hundreds of years ago. In the midst of the Black Lives Matter movement, the climate revolution, and the fall of race-based logos and branding, it's clear that America is changing.

In this book, we will discuss the beginning of the written word. This written word includes the creation of the Cherokee syllabary and the following *Cherokee Phoenix*, the first newspaper published in a Native American language. We will travel from the shores of Virginia, with the great ships on the horizon, to the insides of cozy log cabins where smallpox-infected Cherokee lay dying. We will talk about when war was on the horizon, both within the shores of the United States and across the ocean. We will start with the formation of the Thirteen Colonies and the beginning of the end of Native sovereignty, although this was not the beginning of the Cherokee.

Chapter 1 – Ani'-Yûñ'wiyă'

"[The Native Americans] are really better to us than we are to them; they always give us victuals at their quarters and take care we are armed against hunger and thirst. We do not do so by them (generally speaking), but let them walk by our doors hungry, and do not relieve them. We look upon them with scorn and disdain and think them little better than beasts in humane shape. Though if well examined, we shall find that, for all our religion and education, we possess more moral deformities and evils than these savages do not."

-John Lawson, English settler-colonist in North Carolina, 1709

Before they were the states of Georgia, Alabama, Tennessee, North Carolina, and South Carolina, they were Cherokee territory. Aptly called the "Mountaineers of the South," the Cherokee lived on these forty thousand square miles of lush rivers, skyscraper mountains, and rich forests. Their deep appreciation and respect for nature flourished under these conditions. This lush area in the Appalachian Mountains is called the Blue Ridge. The land provided for them, and they gave back to it in rituals and ceremonies. They also did not abuse the land. The Cherokee followed food as foragers and hunters, but they practiced farming and horticulture as well. The soil quality was not devasted by a majority crop, and the land hosted a wild variety of native plants.

When they grew crops like maize, squash, and beans, they were careful to plant multiple crops in one area. This use of horticulture kept the ground rich with nutrients and the crops thriving. New discoveries led them to find out which plants grew best together and which did not.

Modern farmers are trying to implement the Indigenous way of farming as a way to reverse the effects of over-planting and single-crop devastation.

Many games that the Cherokee played as children were devised to ensure they would be accurate and skilled hunters later in life. For example, one game consisted of players throwing spears at a rolling stone. They also played stickball, which was the origins of modern lacrosse. One of the more famous games is Cherokee marbles, which involves throwing stones or marbles through an L-shaped area.

Due to their placement in the US, the Cherokee hunted elk, bear, and deer. Each piece of the animal was eaten or used. The leather or fur became clothing, the hides were dried as blankets, and the bones were ground for medicine—nothing went to waste.

In the United States, each border has been set with careful intention and is followed according to law. This was not the case a few hundred years ago. There were no borders separating tribal territories. Because of this, these imaginary boundaries were often battlegrounds in the contest for more land to roam. As the largest tribe in the Southeast US, the Cherokee boasted a hefty population of twenty-two thousand people before the 1600s. It is possible they numbered even more, according to new reports.

The word "Cherokee" is of foreign origin and is not the direct translation of Ani'-Yûñ'wiyă', which is what the Cherokee call themselves. The word translates to "the people" or "the real people." There were several different groups of Cherokee. Since membership of their nation was not designated by blood but instead by clan membership, they were split into five separate divisions. Since they occupied such a large portion of the Southeast, each division lived in its own area. There were the Lower Towns, the Middle Towns, the Valley Towns, the Out Towns, and the Overhill Towns. The Lower Towns and the Valley Towns were located in northern Georgia, while the rest were mostly in Tennessee.

The Cherokee lived in log cabins that had a door and a smoke hole in the roof but no windows. Before this, they lived in wattle and daub homes. It is thought that they may have lived in caves before inventing these newer homes. They used stone tools such as knives, chisels, and axes to hunt and create. They also made pottery and woven baskets. Each town had between thirty and forty cabins, as well as a council house, where they would gather and meet.

However, Native Americans did not own land, at least not in the way that Western society does now. Many believed that they belonged to the land, not the other way around. Crowfoot, the chief of the Blackfeet, once said, "Our land is more valuable than your money. It will last forever...We cannot sell the lives of men and animals; therefore we cannot sell this land. It was put here for us by the Great Spirit and we cannot sell it because it does not belong to us." The cessions of land that followed the European invasion showed a completely different side of Native American history. Before, the right to live on the land was fought for and then occupied. After the Europeans came, land was money, and in order to survive, the tribes were often forced into displacement or cession treaties until nothing remained for them at all.

> "You ask me to plow the ground. Shall I take a knife and tear my mother's bosom? You ask me to cut grass and make hay and sell it and be rich like white men. But dare I cut off my mother's hair?"

-Anonymous Native American, 1880s

In this quotation, the struggle between the European cultures and the Native American cultures is glaringly obvious. For the Cherokee, the land was something to live off and give back to. They grew food to support themselves and to trade with fellow tribes, although not to the extent that the Europeans did. They only hunted what they needed and considered overkilling to be wrong. European society centered around the constant need for more, more, more. There's a phrase floating around nowadays that rings true for the 21st century and the 17th century: over-consumption is not sustainable. The Native American tribes practiced conservative farming, hunting, and foraging, making them the poster child for sustainability. Their deep respect for the land and the nature surrounding them allowed for a symbiotic relationship.

However, this relationship faltered and ultimately changed when the European colonists came to their shores. Instead of respecting the land and working in harmony with it, the soil and land were eventually used for profit. It could also be owned, toiled, and depleted without grief or harm. These principles differed so greatly from the Indigenous practices, and this cultural takeover harmed the land as well as the Native American tribes.

The Native American tribes have an incredibly rich and fascinating culture. One thing that stands out, especially when compared to European societies, is the lack of strong alcohol. The Cherokee and other Eastern tribes made alcohol out of fermented berries. Of course, they had tobacco (which is different from the tobacco stuffed in cigarettes today) and other substances used at celebrations and other rituals to elevate the mind. However, since they never drank alcohol with a high alcohol percentage, when the settlers landed and shared a drink with them, a great reckoning occurred. Without a build-up of generational tolerance, the Natives' blood was especially receptive to alcohol, and many quickly grew addicted. This spurred on many trading deals with the settlers. Modern studies have shown that the rates of alcoholism are much higher in Native American populations than in Caucasian or other groups. A study published in 2008 reported that 12 percent of Native deaths (both American and Alaskan or First Nations) were alcohol related.

As their interactions with the Europeans increased, the Cherokee attire changed. Before contact with them, their attire consisted of buckskin clothing adorned with shells and different colored beads. After the settlers arrived and began trading, they continued wearing buckskin leggings but added shirts made of European cloth.

The Cherokee practice many celebrations and rituals throughout the year, with the Sun Dance being one of them. Currently, the Cherokee Nation makes a point not to share details of their traditions with the world, as they are sacred and private. This is also done out of respect for the Cherokee who do still practice these customs and do not wish to have the judgmental eyes of the world on them, especially since these practices were ripped away from them not too long ago.

The Cherokee and other Natives' ways of life were very different from the Europeans. So, when the colonists arrived, a great shift occurred. The first documented case of a settler interacting with Natives in what would one day be the United States took place in the early 1500s. Flash forward a hundred years later, and the settlers had fully arrived.

So, how exactly did the Europeans justify colonizing the New World? The answer lies here: *domitus cultoribus orbis*—"to dominate and conquer the world." The Doctrine of Discovery was created by Pope Alexander VI way back in 1493. This doctrine was a group of 15th-century papal bulls, which means decrees or charters issued by a pope. It decreed that all non-Christian land was *terra nullius* or "empty land." This international law dictated that non-Christian peoples were amoral, barbarous, and subhuman. This granted all Christians, especially missionaries and those who wished to convert, the right and ability to conquer all land and all peoples in the name of Christianity.

> "Among other works well pleasing to the Divine Majesty and cherished of our heart, this assuredly ranks highest, that in our times especially the Catholic faith and the Christian religion be exalted and be everywhere increased and spread, that the health of souls be cared for and that barbarous nations be overthrown and brought to the faith itself."
>
> -Pope Alexander VI, 1493

The current narrative surrounding the reason why settlers came to the US is not entirely correct. These "plantations of religion," including New Jersey, Pennsylvania, and Maryland, served their purpose for Protestants and Catholics alike. However, their ability to come into this land and conquer it for their own use originally came from a Catholic pope. This doctrine allowed them to invade, capture, and subdue non-Christians, as well as "reduce their persons to perpetual slavery." It gave Christians the power to "take away all their possessions and property," not to mention the ability to "convert" the people and the land. Of course, not every settler coming to the New World sought to do this, but the doctrine helped to soothe the people's souls that what they were doing had once been ordained by the pope himself.

Without the Christian idea that only Christians ascend to heaven or that all who do not believe must be converted, the settlers would have had to face their own morality while murdering the Native peoples and stealing their land. As John Lawson, an English colonist, once wrote, "Though if well examined, we shall find that, for all our religion and education, we possess more moral deformities and evils than these savages do not." Sadly, the remnants of this doctrine remain today in US Supreme Court decisions, debates surrounding religious freedom, and the way the Native American population has been oppressed by the federal government.

In order to fully understand American history, we must pay attention to the Native stories. Instead of viewing the past from a Western perspective, we need to put ourselves in the shoes of the Indigenous peoples who were here first. Imagine having a deep knowledge of the land you're on, an understanding of the bark of an oak tree, where the river leads, and what plants are edible or not. This kind of knowledge takes years, generations, or even centuries to amass. So, when a ship lands on your shores, bringing a group of settlers with different ideas, cultures, and norms, what do you do?

Imagine being forced out of your own land because you are barbarous by the invaders' standards. Imagine being handed blankets to keep warm but later realizing they were infected with smallpox and caused an outbreak in your town. Imagine losing those centuries of history and knowledge because this land was farmable, full of timber, and conquerable from a Christian perspective.

When we look at America's current state of affairs, it's interesting to think how the Native American way of life could have prevented the current crises we face. The climate crisis grows nearer and nearer every day, affecting those who live on the coast, bringing harsher heatwaves to the west and more numerous hurricanes to the south. Poison caused by agricultural pesticides and fertilizers seeps into our water towers. Homelessness is abundant. These questions may seem futile, but they reveal a deeper truth. The problems the US faces now possibly could have been prevented generations back by simply respecting the land and its original peoples.

American history books need to change their perspective. Without representing the Native point of view, the education system forgets the original peoples of this country. Without Native American books, stories, and knowledge, the US can push aside its past and continue with inadvisable practices and the need for more. This book aims to change that.

Chapter 2 – Early Conflicts with the European Settlers

"This war did not spring up on our land, this war was brought upon us by the children of the Great Father who came to take our land without a price, and who, in our land, do a great many evil things...This war has come from robbery —from the stealing of our land."

Spotted Tail, Brulé Lakota Chief

In the early 17th century, the Cherokee began trading with the European immigrants, especially the British. This early bond would both serve and destroy them in the future. By the 1650s, the Cherokee had begun to cultivate peaches and watermelon, the seeds of which they acquired through trade deals. The Cherokee were able to trade animal skins, buckskin hides, and beeswax, as well as knowledge of the land. By the 1690s, the Cherokee were often making trade deals with the British in Charles Towne (now Charleston) in what is today the state of South Carolina.

When the Province of Carolina was founded in 1670, trade quickly became not just more popular but also absolutely necessary. The Cherokee culture and economy transformed into what was essentially a market economy. They were originally focused solely on subsistence, keeping their people fed and safe on the land. There was no need to make a profit or rise in the ranks.

However, after realizing how popular animal skins were, they grew into a small commercial empire. Women prepared the skins in advance so the men could sell more at the next trade. And animal skins weren't the only hot commodity. The European settlers brought steel and iron pots and utensils with them, which the Cherokee traded for. This led to a decline in pottery weaving and basket making. Soon enough, copper and stone utensils and tools were completely replaced by steel and iron. As mentioned before, the English brought liquor with them, specifically in the form of whiskey and rum. These spirits also became very popular trading items.

Eventually, after years of trade and a need to remain economically sound, the Cherokee were forced to rely on their trade with the English to stay afloat. This led to an alliance formed with the English and a continuation of trade deals. In the 1690s, the Cherokee repeatedly met with the British in Charles Towne to fight for their basic rights and object to the Europeans' attempted enslavement of their people.

Before the Europeans arrived, the Cherokee, due to their large territory and access to many rivers, had many interactions and alliances with other Native American tribes, especially that of the Creeks. However, after the English arrived and their trade deals commenced, the relationships between tribes grew more and more contentious. Each tribe wanted dominance over trade, and this proved to be fatal.

The Yamasee War in 1715 is such an example. The Yamasee tribe and their allies waged war against the Province of South Carolina due to the settlers' trading abuses and theft of land. The Yamasee land was being encroached on, making their reason for war justified—a situation that happened throughout all of time and around the world. At first, many of the Native American tribes, the Cherokee included, sided with the Yamasee. However, around 1716, the Cherokee switched sides and fought for the British. This rapid shift is a testament to how important trade with the British was becoming to the Cherokee. After asserting their alliance to the British, the Cherokee murdered a group of Creeks who were devoted to the Yamasee cause. Tribal feuds only increased, as well as tensions between the settlers and the Native Americans, as the years went on.

In 1721, the Cherokee ceded land northwest of Charleston to South Carolina. This marks the first official land cession between the Cherokee and the settlers. Sadly, it would not be the last. This deal not only ceded some Cherokee land to the newly formed colony of South Carolina (it was created in 1712) but also regulated trade and introduced a very European idea. This treaty set a strict boundary between the European colonists and the Cherokee. Unlike before, where tribal boundaries were loose and defined by battle, now there was an established border, like what states have now.

A little less than a decade later, a small group of Cherokee leaders traveled across the Atlantic Ocean to visit the king of England. Moytoy of Tellico, also known as Amo-adawehi or "Rainmaker," was the "Emperor of the Cherokee." He gained this title after Sir Alexander Cumming, a trade envoy, had him crowned in order to gain more power, both over them and from the king. Despite being the "official" emperor of the Cherokee (although he was often called king in written reports), Moytoy declined Cumming's offer to take him to England to meet the king. He claimed his wife was ill, so Attakullakulla took his place. About ten others traveled with him to meet King George II.

The Treaty of Whitehall (also known as the Articles of Friendship and Commerce), which was officiated in 1730, followed this meeting. After a stay of four months, the Cherokee traveled home after signing their allegiance to King George II and naming him the true protector of the Cherokee. King George II sent word to the Cherokee delegation, Moytoy specifically, afterward, thanking them for their allegiance and devoted friendship. In part, he said, "The Great King, and the Cherokee Indians, being thus fast'ned together by ye Chain of Friendship, He has ordered his people and children ye English in Carolina to trade with ye Indians, and to furnish them with all manner of goods that they want, and to make hast to build houses, and to plant corn...For he desires that ye Indian and English may live together, as ye children of one family, where ye Great King is a kind of loving Father."

As you can see, the king decrees his lasting friendship with the Cherokee, as well as privileges since they were to be treated as his allies. Apart from the promises of land, trade, and corn, King George II asked one more thing of the Cherokee. Since they were his allies, they were to protect the king and his men from any enemy, whether they be Native or European.

This allegiance served the English well several times in the future. The French and Indian War, which lasted from 1754 to 1763, was one of the many theaters of the Seven Years' War. The French and English were desperate for more land and power, and they began to clash over what is now the state of Ohio, although the war involved all of the northeastern United States as well as Canada. As the Articles of Friendship and Commerce decreed, the Cherokee were now compelled to defend the British and attack the French. It is speculated that almost one-third of the Cherokee force joined the British on the battlefront against the French. This number could have amounted to almost one thousand Cherokee warriors.

Despite their allegiance, issues soon arose. By 1759, the Cherokee had been fighting for several long years. They soon began plundering European settlers to compensate for the lack of funds from the British. Battles and murders ensued, which soon led to war between the former allies.

The Anglo-Cherokee War, which lasted from 1759 to 1761, was brief but deadly. The Cherokee continued attacking settlers while plundering and pillaging the southernmost colonies. The British reacted with only two military invasions that devasted the Cherokee towns. The British set whole towns ablaze, including fields brimming with crops and potential. The British invasions sent Cherokee people running, making them refugees in their own land. These displaced persons were soon ravaged by a smallpox outbreak that diminished their population significantly.

These conflicts gutted the Cherokee more than the English. Only after years of re-population and mending their towns did the Cherokee people resemble what they were before. Despite their warring past, the Cherokee faced yet another potentially disastrous decision when the American Revolutionary War came along. They were still dependent on the English for trade deals and supplies, but great tension was in the air. Originally, most of the Cherokee wanted to stay out of the war. They voted in favor of neutrality again and again. However, by 1776, that majority was overruled, and the Cherokee joined the war to fight with the British against the southern colonies. Perhaps one event that influenced their decision was the King's Proclamation in 1763, which curbed colonial expansion in favor of the Native Americans. Although it was not well enforced or heeded by many settlers, his word could have mattered more to the Cherokee.

The Cherokee fought the colonists from 1776 to 1794. They continued fighting like they had in the Anglo-Cherokee War: attacking settlers in the southeast. All frontier settlements between Cherokee and colonist territory felt the tribe's blows. However, it was nothing compared to what the southern militias did in return.

Just like the British, they burned Cherokee territory to the ground. Almost simultaneously, they managed to scorch entire towns in every region and leave few survivors behind. This loss created even more conflict among the Cherokee. What could be done now? Abandon the British and fight for peace with the Americans? Or simply continue to defend the British?

Dragging Canoe, the head of the Chickamauga Cherokee, decided to stay with the British. Their war lasted for decades, long after the Treaty of Paris ended the war for the British. Eventually, they were forced to back down, but the aftershock of the fatalities, burnt homes, and pillaged communities would be felt for years to come. With the Cherokees divided based on alliances, they were headed into the future on an unstable footing.

Chapter 3 – A Time of Treaties and Compromises

"When a white army battles Indians and wins, it is called a great victory, but if they lose, it is called a massacre."

Chikaskia, Shawnee

Conflict and turmoil infected the New World. Just like the smallpox-infected blankets (most, if not all, were most likely distributed without knowledge of the infection), the lust for war was difficult to banish. Skirmishes on frontier lines, battles between settlements, and wars between tribes ran amuck. The Revolutionary War only helped to spur on this new onset of violence. And the Cherokee were caught in the middle of it.

Although their decision to side with the English a few decades prior had proved to be resourceful and occasionally helpful, the Revolutionary War destroyed the alliance. After fighting against the newly coined American people, the Cherokee were essentially living in enemy territory. The consequences of their past decisions were abundant, affecting their population, territory, and culture. These long-lasting effects helped to cultivate the environment and culture that surrounded the Cherokee. They started off on the wrong foot, and they found themselves hard-pressed to make it up to the new sovereign people.

Think back to the revolutionary period of American history. What was valued most at that time? What was money worth? What resources were valuable? The Cherokee were faced with similar questions. Their utter defeat not only depleted their population but also depleted their options. Without the people needed to fight back, the Cherokee were faced with a tough choice: continue the fight against the Americans or assimilate and apologize as needed. The Cherokee chose the latter. The American War for Independence granted independence to a very specific group of people. The rest were desperate to blend in.

There were several treaties over the course of a decade or so that significantly cut into Cherokee territory. This list includes the Treaty of Sycamore Shoals (1775), the Treaty of DeWitt's Corner (1777), and the Treaty of Long Island of Holston (1777), just to name a few.

The first of these treaties was the Treaty of Sycamore Shoals. This treaty was not forged in war or defeat, so the Cherokee had an unusual—but still little—amount of power in the negotiation. This deal was put into place by the Overhill Cherokee and the European settlers in Kentucky. The Cherokee agreed to sell a very large swath of land that is now in central Kentucky. Regardless of whether they needed the money, trade deals, or felt intimidated into signing this treaty, their land was still slowly being encroached upon. Just as an endless tide erodes the shoreline, so the settlers lessened the Cherokees' land.

The Treaty of DeWitt's Corner served as a way to end the Cherokee War, which was sparked and ended (for the most part) during the American Revolutionary War. In essence, the Cherokee lost to South Carolina. With their homes and land burned and ruined, the Cherokee people needed to create some kind of peace with the European settlers. However, this treaty was dictated by the winners, as much of history is, so the Cherokee did not have much power. The Treaty of DeWitt's Corner took nearly all of the Cherokee territory in South Carolina and decreed American laws would take precedent over Cherokee law in trade and other such encounters.

What followed were two treaties that were essentially sibling treaties. These two different treaties, very similar in name and nature, continued to limit Cherokee power and encroach on their territory. They were the Treaty of Long Island of Holston, signed in 1777, and then the Treaty of the Holston, which was signed a little under two decades later, 1791, to be specific. We will start with the Treaty of Long Island of Holston.

In 1777, things were not going well for the Cherokee. As discussed above, siding with the British took a very quick turn for the worst and left the Cherokee dismantled. During this period, Cherokee territory was inhabited by not only the Cherokee but also white Europeans, especially in what is modern-day Tennessee. By signing the Treaty of Long Island of Holston, the Cherokee agreed to give up their power over the territory in eastern Tennessee that the settlers lived on.

Flash forward several years. The Revolutionary War had been won by the settlers, and the British were sent back across the ocean, sullen and defeated. Promise hung in the air for the new American people, but the Cherokee weren't filled with the same joy. As mentioned above, their choice to side with the British left them in a dangerous position at the end of the war. This treaty was simply one example of that danger.

In 1785, just two years after the war had officially ended, the Treaty of New Hopewell was created and signed. Despite the carefully worded language of this treaty, the premise and promise of it remain clear to this day. The Cherokee were now under the power of the federal government of the United States of America, at least to some extent. All trade was to be regulated and supervised by the American government. The Cherokee trade deals with the British were long gone.

The final article of the Treaty of Hopewell states:

> "The hatchet shall be forever buried, and the peace given by the United States, and friendship re-established between the said states on the one part, and all the Cherokees on the other, shall be universal; and the contracting parties shall use their utmost endeavors to maintain the peace given as aforesaid, and friendship re-established."

The word "friendship" is used heavily in Article XIII, but its definition is never clearly stated. The Cherokee were granted the right to elect deputies who could communicate with Congress about their needs and trade deals. However, as Article IX states, "the United States in Congress assembled shall have the sole and exclusive right of regulating the trade with the Indians, and managing all their affairs in such manner as they think proper."

As per usual, this treaty also further established new boundaries between the Cherokee and the American people. It also states that the Cherokee could deal with people who sought to settle their lands as they saw fit, something that later did not sit well with settlers. As well, it decrees that all Americans living on Cherokee territory (except for a certain settlement that was still up in the air at that point) must leave within six months' time.

This treaty marks a very distinctive transition in the history of the Cherokee people. The Treaty of New Hopewell was just the beginning of a long and slanderous history of what we have come to call genocide, improper governance, and loss of power for the Cherokee. In truth, it was not the beginning. This began the moment the settlers set foot on the shores of the Americas and used the papal bull to declare their God-given power over the Native peoples. Fear crept in for the Cherokee. They were faced with a seemingly impossible task: how can one blend in with a country and culture that hasn't even been created yet? And if this wasn't enough, how can a person give up the culture and practices that have been a part of their people for thousands of years?

Flash forward to 1791. The Cherokee had been assimilating under the American power and influence. The Treaty of the Holston, the sequel to the Treaty of Long Island of Holston, now comes into play. For one of the first times in American history, the rhetoric surrounding "civilizing" the Natives emerged. This treaty asks for "permanent peace and friendship...and to remove the causes of war, by ascertaining [Cherokee] limits and making other necessary, just and friendly arrangements." Once again, the federal government emphasized peace and friendship with the Cherokee only to backtrack by setting intense and unjust rules and boundaries on its relationship with them.

This "perpetual peace" could be achieved, or so Governor William Blount of Ohio thought, by the Cherokee ceding more territory, specifically the region south of the Ohio River. As a gift to the Cherokee for giving up their land and staying out of it (relinquishing all claims they had), the government agreed to pay one thousand dollars annually to the chiefs and warriors. Just like the Treaty of Hopewell, the Treaty of the Holston further reinforced that the US would be the only trading partner with the Cherokee. The government would also regulate and control all trade between the two.

Article XIV introduces the concept of civilizing the Cherokee:

> "That the Cherokee nation may be led to a greater degree of civilization, and to become herdsman and cultivators, instead of remaining in a state of hunters, the United States will from time to time furnish gratuitously the said nation with useful implements of husbandry, and further to assist the said nation in so desirable a pursuit, and at the same time to establish a certain mode of

communication, the United States will send such... who shall qualify themselves to act as interpreters."

This article is only the beginning of a long and sordid history of attempting to "civilize" the Native peoples in the United States. The federal government wished for the Cherokee to become more settled, as this would further civilize and assimilate them. The need for the Cherokee to become a part of the Western Christian world, which would, therefore, make them less of a threat, would only grow as the years passed. Even in the 20th century, laws were passed banning Native American dances, rituals, and ceremonies from taking place. This practice of stripping them of their culture lasted long after the 1780s.

In 1804, four treaties were signed at Tellico. All of them had to do with land cessions on the Cherokees' part. The Cherokee were paid fairly well, all things considered, but the encroachment on their land only continued. With nowhere else to go, the Cherokee were faced with yet another impossible challenge. They continued making deals with the United States government, mostly out of need and intimidation. They relied on them for trade and economic developments, as they weren't allowed to make trade deals with individual states or foreign sovereign powers.

During this great transitional period, the Cherokee were forced to make a decision. And they did. In the following years, the Cherokee tribes attempted to assimilate and blend into the newborn American culture as best they could. But it still wasn't enough.

Chapter 4 – The Assimilation of the Cherokee

"The American Indian is of the soil, whether it be the region of forests, plains, pueblos, or mesas. He fits into the landscape, for the hand that fashioned the continent also fashioned the man for his surroundings. He once grew as naturally as the wild sunflowers, he belongs just as the buffalo belonged."

- Luther Standing Bear, Oglala Sioux Chief

The end of the Revolutionary War and the sudden onslaught of treaties had the Cherokee embarking on a brand-new journey. After being defeated and forced to sell or simply cede their land, the Cherokee decided to try to assimilate. They were one of the most successful tribes when it came to blending in, but, as we will see later in their tale, their effort was not enough for them to remain in the East.

After the Articles of the Confederation failed, the US federal government wrote the Constitution of the United States in 1787, ratified it in 1788, and put it into place in 1789. This new document became an integral part of the Native American communities. First and foremost, it recognized all Native tribes as nations within the United States and "declared that all treaties with them were part of 'the Supreme Law of the Land.'" This sudden declaration instilled hope within the Cherokee community. There was a chance now that the former treaties would never be revisited, revised, or erased. As well, there was a chance that there would be no need for new ones. The Cherokee would finally be allowed to live and let be.

This new decree was the final push to force the Cherokee to blend in with the new American culture. Their assimilation led them to create their own system of law and order in 1808. These guards, essentially the Cherokee policing system, began operating in the late 1790s but weren't named and fully established until the 1820s. Their original name was the Light Horsemen, which later evolved into the Light Horse Guards. Their duty was to preserve peace among the Cherokee, not to mention preventing all sorts of crimes, including murder, rape, theft, and intoxication. The Light Horse Guards' duties were incredibly similar to the police force that currently serves the United States. There are still some very obvious differences, however. The Light Horsemen often operated under the stealth of night, rubbing themselves with tobacco to appear invisible. In addition, some of their laws were sworn into place with sacred rituals and ceremonies, with what we would today associate with magic. Many Light Horsemen were also sorcerers, and they were known in their clans for having great powers.

These sharp differences make for a very interesting historical evolution. However, it's important to note how beautiful this blend of cultures became. The Cherokee ardently attempted to assimilate, to adopt these European traditions and integrate their own culture with them. This forced conformity was a truly terrible act. However, the Cherokee managed to perform and conform with grace and ease. The need to survive on the land that was once theirs gave them the strength to adapt to the surrounding culture and find ways to practice their own traditions.

The United States has always been referred to as a "melting pot," a place where cultures, nationalities, and ethnicities combine. As is noted in hundreds of textbooks, manuscripts, and letters, the blending of cultures did not always go smoothly. Skirmishes broke out between different European cultures before the settlers could all identify as "American." Even now, the word "American" has expanded to include "Asian American," "African American," or "Arab American." This inclusion of culture was not granted to the Cherokee. That being said, hardships were faced by all immigrants coming into the United States. However, the need to erase the Native American culture, to have them embrace Christian and European concepts and traditions, predates the struggles faced by the many peoples to come.

The Cherokee became farmers and Protestants, feeling European American encroachment and the need to assimilate. There was talk amongst the federal officials about "civilizing" the Native Americans or, in simpler terms, to give them a faith that they all believed in. Protestant missionaries began a campaign to convert the Natives, which the US hoped could eventually be used to control the Native American tribes better. In the meantime, the culture around them continued to change.

In 1810, the Cherokee people abolished clan revenge. Clan revenge was very similar to the blood feuds that occurred during the time of *Beowulf*. Clan revenge, also referred to as blood revenge, acted as their legal system, or at least the base of it. If a member of one clan killed a member of the other, it was the sworn duty of the victim's clan to exact revenge. This could be done in one of two ways. They could kill the murderer, or the killer's clan could offer up another life for them to take. The latter option was a little more complicated, but it often ceased all future conflict. If the victim's clan were to pick the second choice, the other clan would not be able to take revenge on them for that death. However, if the deaths continued, clan revenge could quickly escalate into a full-on blood feud.

There were very specific rules in regard to clan revenge, such as only a relative could avenge the deceased. If such rules weren't obeyed, then the following murder would not end the revenge; in fact, it would begin another. However, a murder that occurred in self-defense was not a cause for blood revenge. In its very essence, clan revenge was just "an eye for an eye."

So, when the Cherokee abolished blood revenge, a very distinctive shift in tribal history took place. Clearly, change had arrived on their doorstep. Blood feuds and clan revenge were so ingrained in their history and culture that abolishing it left a gaping hole in their society. To fill its place, the Cherokee adopted a new legal system, one that was widely based on the US federal government. The Cherokee National Supreme Court was formed in 1820. This administration had eight judicial districts, each representing a different Cherokee clan.

However, the change didn't stop there. Just a few years later, a soldier who served in the Creek War alongside the US Army named Sequoyah created the Cherokee syllabary. A syllabary is like an alphabet in that it is a written version of a language. However, a syllabary has one symbol per syllable, while alphabets do not. Before this, all Native American tribes in

North America communicated orally. History and stories were passed down through oral tradition, not through the written word. Modern and ancient historians rely on the written word to track a group of people and the events of history. The oral tradition did not fit into Western historians' mindset, and so, it was often forgotten about. They followed the paper trail, not the words spoken between grandparent and child.

Sequoyah revolutionized the Cherokee people, though it wasn't an easy feat. Over the course of twelve years, he created this syllabary, and his effort allowed the Cherokee to remain a united front in the face of assimilation. There are around eighty-five symbols within the Cherokee syllabary. The Cherokee Nation officially adopted Sequoyah's incredible invention in 1825.

Sequoyah's great revolution spurred on a remarkable series of events. The Cherokee adopted a written constitution thanks to him, and their sudden literacy allowed religious literature to become far more popular. Finally, in February of 1828, the *Cherokee Phoenix* was published. This was the first Native American newspaper ever. The *Cherokee Phoenix* is now known for publishing stories that raise attention to Native problems and issues that they solely face. This newspaper continued printing until 1834 when they were temporarily shut down due to a lack of funding. The *Cherokee Phoenix* was reborn as the *Cherokee Advocate* in 1975. Finally, in 2007, they returned to the original name, the *Cherokee Phoenix*.

Let's go back a few years. The Cherokee had undergone serious changes and transitions within the past century, such as the constant overturn of sovereignty, loss of territory, famine, smallpox epidemics, and the creation of a brand-new culture and society. After siding with the English backfired, the Cherokee began to make their new allegiance known. During the Battle of Horseshoe Bend, the Cherokee tribe helped General Andrew Jackson, who would eventually become the seventh president of the United States, fight the Red Sticks, a faction of the Creek tribe that broke away to challenge the US government. Around five hundred Cherokee helped Jackson defeat the Red Sticks on March 27th, 1814. This battle led to the end of the Creek War, which lasted from 1813 to 1814.

Although this battle was with the Creek (mainly the Red Sticks), the American soldiers would plunder and raid Cherokee villages just the same. However, the Cherokee fought ardently for General Jackson. They suffered at least fifty casualties (both dead and wounded) in that battle alone.

However, the Battle of Horseshoe Bend was more significant for the Cherokee. Once the battle had been won, General Andrew Jackson promised friendship and peace to the Cherokee. General Jackson was quoted as saying, "As long as the sun shines and the grass grows there shall be friendship between us, and the feet of the Cherokee shall be toward the East." Imagine after a century of land encroachment, rigged treaties, and forcible removal from your land, a general with power and respect promises that your feet, your people, and your tribe will always remain in the East, where they belong. Did the Cherokee sigh a breath of relief then? Did they wonder if this would finally be the end of the chaos? Jackson's promise justified their assimilation. His words made it all seem worth it. If all they had to do was pledge allegiance to the flag, adopt the new American culture, and continue to farm the land, then there was hope for them after all.

Their efforts to blend into American society went without much acknowledgment. Despite their hard work and sacrifice, the Native Americans, in general, were always ranked last on the list of priorities. Although Jackson's words held some merit, as did the treaties, they had all been broken in the past. Promises could be betrayed with one action, and treaties could be forgotten if new resources were discovered. The Cherokee entered this new era as a tired but hopeful nation, fighting for their existence and their right to remain in the East.

Chapter 5 – The Beginnings of the Great Removal

"We, the great mass of the people think only of the love we have for our land, we do love the land where we were brought up. We will never let our hold to this land go, to it go it will be like throwing away the mother that gave birth."

- Aitooweyah writing to Principal Chief Ross

When we look back at American history as a whole, there are several defining events—moments that forever stained the nation, moments that had a ripple effect and changed the future, and moments that will never be forgotten. Whether historians like to admit it or not, there is a tendency to push these moments under the rug. Some of them, such as the American War for Independence or Lincoln's profound address at Gettysburg, are monumentalized and iconized. These moments have become staples in humanities discussions, history classes, and textbooks. These monumental moments are deserving of their status in our society, as their changes were felt for years to come.

However, what is often forgotten, pushed under the rug, or sugarcoated are the moments that defined the United States in the most terrible of ways. It is important to recognize that this kind of thing happens in every country. These are the moments where neighbor turns against neighbor, where human life is not valued, or where the right to happiness, freedom, and joy is given based on the color of skin or one's status. These are the more sinister aspects of our history as a whole, the ones we wish we could forget about it and the ones that we're ashamed to know that our ancestors took part in.

These moments can make our skin crawl. They're not easy to listen to, read about, or talk about. But if we are to understand our history, we must recognize these moments. Learning about them is not only a necessity to fully comprehend the course of time, but it is also necessary to prevent such moments from ever happening again.

Now, let's get into it, shall we? After spending much of the late 1700s and early 1800s adjusting to this new America and successfully assimilating, the Cherokee were betrayed. President Andrew Jackson was in office from 1829 to 1837. He completed a series of two terms during which he accomplished much of what he said he was going to in his campaign. However, some of his accomplishments tarnished American history and decimated the Cherokee people.

One year into his stay as president, Jackson signed the Indian Removal Act into law. This came as a great surprise to the Cherokee people. The year 1830 was a mere fifteen years after the Battle of Horseshoe Bend, that same battle where Jackson had promised the Cherokee that their people would forever stay on their rightful ancestral land. The Indian Removal Act essentially stripped his words of their value and dissolved all remaining hope for the Cherokee. This law gave the acting president the power to move the Native domains westward, as well as their people. The president was now able to forcibly remove the Cherokee people legally. President Jackson agreed that all Native Americans needed to be removed and transplanted somewhere west of the Mississippi.

But why this sudden change of heart? Less than two decades prior, President Jackson had been grateful for their service in his campaign. Something changed in his time between general and president. It was the sudden discovery of gold and the fertile land ripe for growing cotton. These findings pockmark American history like stormy clouds in a clear, blue sky. This was not the first, nor the last time Native Americans would be forcibly evicted from their land due to the discovery of plentiful natural resources.

Gold was found in Georgia on Cherokee territory. Although the Cherokee had ceded most of their land in Georgia, they still retained a small portion. This discovery pushed the federal government to make some harsh decisions. After all, they had no right to that land so long as the Cherokee laid claim to it. The only solution they could think of was to remove them, grant them land elsewhere, and then exploit the land themselves.

This shows the great difference between the Native American cultures and the European cultures. The Native Americans lived in respect and accordance with the land, only hunting as needed and using every morsel of the animal. Nothing went to waste. They did not drill into the land for materials or mine for gold. In fact, they believed they did not own the land. Instead, they belonged to the land.

One famous Native American proverb goes as follows: "Treat the earth well: it was not given to you by your parents, it was loaned to you by your children. We do not inherit the Earth from our Ancestors, we are borrowing it from our children." Unlike the European Americans, this land was not their God-given right. The Native Americans lived in harmony with it, which made the land rich in resources and ripe for harvest.

It should be of no great surprise then that when such valuable resources were discovered, the Americans were quick to rush in and take it. President Jackson did not live up to his promise to the Cherokee people; instead, he ordered one of the most heinous acts in the history of the United States: The Trail of Tears.

In 1835, a little after gold was discovered in modern-day Georgia, the Treaty of New Echota was signed by both the Cherokee and the US government. Essentially, the Americans were desperate for the gold-enriched land and were ready to pay or do anything to get it. The Cherokees, on the other hand, were hesitant to sell or cede any more of their land, as it had already been lessened quite a bit. However, the Cherokee ended up selling all their land east of the Mississippi River for five million dollars, which was a hefty sum back then. But the majority of the Cherokee vehemently opposed the Treaty of New Echota. The few who supported the Treaty of New Echota and signed in its favor were committed and tried for treason.

John Ross was the principal chief of the Cherokee Nation at that time. He served as principal chief from 1828 to 1866, the year of his death. Chief Ross was of Scottish and Cherokee descent, and he originally served as a translator and diplomat between the Cherokee Nation and the US Army. He was later promoted to the Cherokee National Council and finally rose to the role of principal chief of the Cherokee Nation. He was a staunch and ardent supporter of Cherokee rights and advocated for their stay in the East.

After the US declared its intentions to secure the gold underneath the Cherokees' feet, Chief Ross wrote a letter declaring his disappointment and disgust with the new treaty proposed by the federal government. He details the betrayal the Cherokee felt when the treaty was presented, claiming that though they may have once been considered American citizens or at least guardians of the state, they were now only strangers. Chief Ross also notes how many people protested against the Indian Removal Act—over fifteen thousand people did so—and how the federal government would never obtain their consent. His words hold the pressing urgency that the Cherokee felt at the time, as well as the knowledge that they were facing a crossroads.

His dedication to his people and their rights is as clear and pure as crystalline water. His call to action led the Cherokee to pursue legal justice. The Cherokee faced little trouble in the way of the courts. They were in luck; since only a minority had signed, the majority was able to refute it and take their case to the United States Supreme Court.

In a very interesting turn of events, the Supreme Court ruled in favor of the majority. Their ruling stated that Georgia had no right to the Cherokee land east of the Mississippi since it wasn't a unanimous decision. This was one of the first times that the federal government ever worked or voted in favor of the Cherokee people. Supreme Court Justice John Marshall was one of the key factors in this decision. His support of the Cherokee gave them hope for a future in the East. He opened his statements by introducing the bill in question, as well as the rights of the Cherokee. Supreme Court Justice John Marshall did not sugarcoat the situation, as he details society being at risk if this removal were to occur. Justice Marshall also detailed the many treaties laid in place by the US in the past and argued that they were still in effect, making any sort of trespassing on their territory illegal under US treaty law.

Supreme Court Justice John Marshall makes it clear within the first few opening statements that the Cherokee attempt to assimilate and make peace with the Americans was reason enough to allow them to stay. However, it's later on when he delves more into the tense treaties that the Cherokee and government had undergone.

> "The condition of the Indians in relation to the United States is perhaps unlike that of any other two people in existence. In the general, nations not owing a common allegiance are foreign to

each other. The term *foreign nation* is, with strict propriety, applicable by either to the other. But the relation of the Indians to the United States is marked by peculiar and cardinal distinctions which exist nowhere else. The Indian Territory is admitted to compose part of the United States...[the Indians] are considered as within the jurisdictional limits of the United States, subject to many of those restraints which are imposed upon our own systems...Though the Indians area acknowledged to have an unquestionable and, heretofore, unquestioned right to the lands they occupy until that right shall be extinguished by a voluntary cession to our government, yet it may well be doubted whether...[the Indians] can, with strict accuracy, be denominated foreign nations. They may more correctly, perhaps, be denominated domestic dependent nations...Their relation to the United States resembles that of a ward to his guardian."

Justice John Marshall clearly states here the difficult-to-describe setting in which the Cherokee (and Native Americans as a whole) and the Americans interact. Their uneven footing within this country, although not in their favor, does prevent such an action from legally happening, or at least from happening with the Supreme Court's position. However, his following statement fully paints the picture of dominance and reliance on Indigenous lands. Justice Marshall spoke of the plight of the Native Americans and their incomparable living situation within the borders of the United States. He spoke of their inability to form connections or alliances with other countries due to their treaties and agreements with the US federal government, which left them in a murky position.

Supreme Court Justice John Marshall not only outlined the incredibly complicated and abstract territorial agreement shared between the Cherokee and the United States. He also took it one step further by detailing the relationship that had since grown from this establishment. Purely because of the European settlers' arriving here, kicking the British monarchy out, and forcing the Natives to only trade with Americans, the Cherokee were reliant on the US Justice Marshall was correct in saying that they were not truly a foreign nation, seeing as they were under American sovereignty but also because they had none of the rights a foreign nation would.

Later on in his remarks, Supreme Court Justice Marshall made it clear that he didn't believe that the Supreme Court truly had the power to address this problem. He said, "If it be true that the Cherokee Nation have rights, this is not the tribunal in which those rights are to be asserted. If it be true that wrongs have been inflicted and that still greater are to be apprehended, this is not the tribunal which can redress the past or prevent the future." These words do not negate the power of the Supreme Court's ruling, but it does cast doubt on the validity and authority behind them. It's fair to wonder if perhaps these two sentences allowed the series of events behind the Trail of Tears to occur or if they were going to happen no matter what. Either way, the ball was set in motion, and this Supreme Court ruling sadly did not do much to stop it.

Although the ruling may look great on paper, it did not translate well into the real world. Yes, the Supreme Court ruled in favor of the Cherokee, as the way they presented their problem was compelling and understandable. However, in the end, President Andrew Jackson ignored the Supreme Court's decision, as did the whole state of Georgia. Together, they conspired against the Cherokee and continued doing as they pleased, no matter the consequences.

Despite the efforts of the Cherokee government, former US Secretary of State Henry Clay, Senator Daniel Webster of Massachusetts, and the Supreme Court ruling, everything soon fell to pieces. President Jackson used his authoritative power as the seventh president of the United States to break his promise to the Cherokee people. Their efforts to assimilate were not enough to retain the right to stay in the East where their ancestors had lived. The establishment of an American-inspired government was not enough, nor was the creation of Sequoyah's syllabary. Despite Americanizing their legal system, police force, and way of life, the Cherokee were still seen as something in the way of the true treasure that lay beneath the surface.

If we follow the trail of US history, picking up the breadcrumbs of the past as we go, several themes emerge. One of these can easily be seen here: the disrespect and sudden lack of value for human life when valuable resources emerge. This can also be seen in the respect for animal life, plant life, and ecosystems around the world. Take deep-sea mining, for example. The computer on which this book was written would not have been possible without the precious metals extracted from the deep-sea floors. However, that extraction wreaks chaos on the ocean floor, disrupts food chains, and causes trauma and death for the creatures that live down there.

These are the sacrifices made for the conveniences we enjoy today. The pursuit of wealth, resources, and material happiness became the foundation of not only American society but also many societies around the world. The Cherokee were simply the victim of it. There's a Lakota saying about the separation between man and nature and the consequences of such a brutal and unnatural divorce. It goes like this: "When a man moves away from nature, his heart becomes hard." When nature becomes a commodity, when land is only something to farm or something to sell, when an animal is only food, and when every living, breathing, and beautiful thing is narrowed down to a single definition, what becomes of man then?

Chapter 6 – The Trail of Tears

"We are now about to take our leave and kind farewell to our native land, the country the Great Spirit gave our Fathers, we are on the eve of leaving that country that gave us birth, it is with sorrow we are forced by the white man to quit the scenes of our childhood...we bid farewell to it and all we hold dear."

- Charles Hicks, Cherokee, November 4, 1838

And so, we have arrived at one of the greatest stains on American history: the Trail of Tears. President Andrew Jackson was elected to his first term in 1829 and finished his last in 1837. Although he was not in office to oversee the entire process, he was the creator and ultimate originator of the Trail of Tears. His successor, Martin Van Buren, and his generals were the overseers of the mass forced exodus of the Cherokee.

Newspapers around the country announced the government's decision, as well as the promotion of General Winfield Scott, who would now lead the Cherokee to the West. In 1838, the first trial of the Trail of Tears began for the Cherokee. They were not the first to leave, though. The Seminoles of Florida had already been forced to leave by this point; however, they put up a bloody fight. This past history of violence and resistance potentially influenced the way the US soldiers treated the Cherokee. The US government began their forcible removal in the early summer, but their fleets of soldiers, volunteers, and camps were vastly underprepared. The Cherokee began dying, with illness, injuries, and violence being prevalent. This absolute failure put the whole mission on pause, which gave the federal government time to recuperate and come up with a new plan.

Principal Chief John Ross of the Cherokee, a fervent opposer to the Indian Removal Act and staunch supporter of Native American rights, began to work with the US government. After seeing how terribly the first attempt had ended, Chief Ross decided to take matters into his own hands. He was asked to figure out an estimated budget for the trip, calculate the time needed for travel, and ways to ration their food.

Chief Ross worked tirelessly as the superintendent of the Cherokee Removal and Subsistence committee. The sheer number of people the US government were trying to move created much bigger problems than it had originally thought of. Not to mention the resistance and force they encountered. When Principal Chief John Ross's budget was presented to the rest of the Cherokee Removal and Subsistence committee, it was rejected. The others cut corners, scaled back his estimations, and gave less than what was truly needed. Despite Ross's efforts, the horrors that had plagued the Cherokee in the summer followed them on the second attempt.

The Cherokee Removal and Subsistence's time spent planning the Trail of Tears let the seasons slip by as quickly as sand. Summer turned to fall, and before they knew it, it was almost winter. The weather was an unwelcome touch of terror. The first week of October of 1838 distilled fear into the hearts of thousands of Cherokees. This was the first week of their historical journey, one that would bring both the Cherokee Nation and the US government to their heels.

The goal was to remove all Cherokee from the East and relocate them westward around or close to what is now the state of Oklahoma (back then, Oklahoma was an unorganized territory). Cherokee slaveholders traveled with their slaves, women held on to their children, and the elderly were forced to walk. Almost no one was left behind. The journey was estimated to take over one hundred days, so they would be forced to travel throughout the fall and winter months. Some of the Cherokee and their slaves traveled barefoot, most with inadequate supplies or just the clothes on their backs.

General Winfield Scott, one of President Martin Van Buren's righthand men, had over seven thousand troops under his command. General Scott was already a known force in Indigenous removal—he had taken part in the attempted Seminole removal as well as the massacre of the Creek. His soldiers were ordered to forcibly remove the Cherokee from the East by whatever means necessary. Many of the Cherokee were forced out of their homes at gunpoint. More than sixteen thousand Cherokee were removed from their communities and stationed in internment camps while the volunteer militia plundered and burned their homes.

However, in the newspaper announcement, General Winfield Scott made sure to say that the Cherokee would be treated with dignity and respect. General Scott claimed that each and every soldier had been ordered to treat the Native Americans with the utmost kindness and respect and that any who chose not to comply could be tried. He even asked his fellow officers and men to watch out for noncompliance and inappropriate behavior and granted them the ability to bring guilty men to court.

He then details the necessary evils that may occur. If someone was relocating an entire family, they should not fire upon them unless resistance occurred. If the family did not cooperate initially, it was considered best to kidnap one member of the family and hope the rest followed along for fear of separation. General Winfield Scott, along with his troops, led thirteen separate groups east, with each group being of a similar size. Other groups were led by Captain John Benge, John Bell, and Chief John Ross. A conservative estimate for the loss of Cherokee life on the Trail of Tears is four thousand. Some historians believe the actual number could be upward of six thousand (and this is only for the Cherokee; this number excludes the other tribes that were forced to move). According to some of the reports from the time, almost twelve Cherokee were buried at each and every stop along the trail. Government reports and documents of the time are misleading and usually false. The true toll might never be known.

There were several paths on the Trail of Tears. Those who traveled north went through Tennessee, Kentucky, Illinois, Missouri, and Arkansas only to finally land in Oklahoma. Other groups dipped down south, trekking through Alabama, the borders of Mississippi, and all the way through Arkansas. Those who took a more direct path went straight through Tennessee and Arkansas. Each trail presented its own problems, whether that be weather, the previous inhabitants, or challenges in the terrain. For those who survived the arduous trail, the final destination was always the same, however: Tahlequah, which would become the new capital of the Cherokee Nation.

John G. Burnett, one of the Cherokee messengers, recorded the following about the Trail of Tears:

> "I saw the helpless Cherokees arrested and dragged from their homes, and driven at the bayonet point into the stockades. And in the chill of a drizzling rain on an October morning I saw them loaded like cattle or sheep into six hundred and forty-five wagons and started toward the west...One can never forget the sadness and solemnity of that morning... The trail of the exiles was a trail of death. They had to sleep in the wagons and on the ground without fire. And I have known as many as twenty-two of them to die in one night of pneumonia due to ill treatment, cold, and exposure...The long painful journey to the west ended March 26th, 1839, with four-thousand silent graves reaching from the foothills of the Smoky Mountains to what is known as the Indian territory in the West. And covetousness on the part of the white race was the cause of all that the Cherokees had to suffer."

Here's another firsthand account from a "Native of Maine," which was detailed in *The New York Observer*:

> "On Tuesday evening we fell into a detachment of the poor Cherokee Indians, about eleven hundred...We found them in the forrest camped for the night...under a severe fall of rain...many of the aged Indians were suffering extremely from the fatigue of the journey, and ill health... We found the road literally filled with a procession for nearly three miles in length...The sick and feeble were carried in wagons...multitudes go on foot—even aged females apparently nearly ready to drop in the grave were traveling with heavy burdens...on the sometimes frozen ground...with no covering for feet...They buried 14 or 15 at every stopping place...some carry a downcast dejected look...of despair, others wild frantic appearance as if to pounce like a tiger upon their enemies..."

The Trail of Tears was rightly named. The effects of this mass removal are still felt by the United States today. General Scott's men managed to remove almost every single Cherokee from their home. Between 400 to 1,500 remained in North Carolina, hiding away in the mountains and on small farms. Some of them were granted permission to stay, as they lived on privately owned land rather than shared land. After the Cherokees' arrival in northeastern Oklahoma in March, they were faced with yet another problem. This territory was already inhabited by the Osage and Cherokee who had traveled here in the past. Feuds and disputes over land rights and boundaries began almost immediately.

However, even the Trail of Tears was pushed under the rug. This horrible act was refuted for so long and often made out to be less than it truly was. In autumn of 1986, *The Wilson Quarterly* published a short article written by W. R. Higginbotham. In it, he claimed that the Trail of Tears was actually not a forcible removal and that the death toll was greatly overexaggerated. Here's what he had to say in "A Dubious 'Trail of Tears'":

> "Twenty-plus years of research in original documents, both U.S. and Cherokee, have convinced me that the story is simply untrue. The Cherokees supplied themselves from U.S. funds agreed upon in advance by Cherokee leaders. No military force accompanied the main groups west.
>
> As for the alleged number of deaths, Cherokee Nation records themselves show that large contingents arrived in Indian territory with more Indians than were counted upon leaving the eastern Cherokee homelands. The groups picked up stragglers on the way. The 4,000-death estimate was by a distraught missionary mourning the loss of an infant before the movement started. Detailed reports elsewhere do not support it.
>
> The phrase 'Trail of Tears' first appeared in 1908, 70 years after the episode. An Oklahoma historian reported it out of the mouth of a Choctaw Indian to a Baptist preacher describing a road in what is now Oklahoma. Historians grabbed onto it like a slogan. The Cherokees never used it."

Higginbotham's blatant denial of the Trail of Tears only supports the truth. As can be seen throughout history, the atrocities committed by countries around the world are forced out of the minds of those who did not suffer, as they are those terrible moments in history that we wish we could forget. Here, Higginbotham twists facts around to make his own view come across as true. Yes, it's true that the Cherokees were granted funds from the US government to complete the move. However, this was also ordered by the federal government, not the Cherokee people. Chief John Ross asked for more funds, rations, and supplies than the government supplied. If anything, the agreement that was made in advance was not honored, as can be seen through the violation of previous treaties that stated the territory belonged to the Cherokee and the Cherokee alone.

Higginbotham also contradicts himself in the second paragraph. The Cherokee were not the only people to travel on the Trail of Tears. Some of the Choctaw and Seminole were forced along the route, as well as their slaves. If they picked up people along the way, it only makes sense that there would be a greater number arriving, even with the death toll. There were already Cherokee and Osage living in Oklahoma at the time, which would account for the sudden crowding in Oklahoma. One tribal displacement led to yet another displacement of more Indigenous peoples.

Higginbotham does not address the potential inaccuracy of the government's reports. Many deaths were not reported along the way, nor did anyone feel a need to do so in the first place. Death became a friend to them, as it followed them along the trail. There was no escaping it. Burying twelve people at every stop would be more than difficult to stomach, much less report. Higginbotham also did not include firsthand accounts, which means his version of the story was based on biased reports and a general misunderstanding. Had he looked at the past, at the patterns in history as a whole, he would have realized the truth.

A simple and innocent discovery forced the Cherokee off their land and expelled them to the west. John G. Burnett describes the moment that everything changed, "In the year 1828, a little Indian boy living on Ward Creek had sold a gold nugget to a white trader, and that nugget sealed the doom of the Cherokees. In a short time, the country was overrun with armed brigands claiming to be government agents...Homes were burned and the inhabitants driven out by the gold-hungry brigands." The insatiable need for wealth, material possessions, and status symbols effectively killed one-quarter of the Cherokee, if not more.

The firsthand reports are clear: the Trail of Tears was one of the greatest atrocities in American history. There is no use in pushing it under the rug, of forgetting the names and lives of those who were killed, or of the great sacrifice made by Chief John Ross's wife, Elizabeth "Quatie," who gave her only blanket to protect a child from the cold. Quatie soon died of pneumonia, as she froze in the night due to a fall of sleet and snow. In honoring their lives and deaths, we must learn of their legacies.

Chapter 7 – An Examination of the Trail of Tears from a Modern Viewpoint

"At this time, 1890, we are too near the removal of the Cherokees for our young people to fully understand the enormity of the crime that was committed against a helpless race. Truth is, the facts are being concealed from the young people of today. School children of today do not know that we are living on lands that were taken from a helpless race at the bayonet point to satisfy the white man's greed...Murder is still murder whether committed by the villain skulking in the dark or by uniformed men stepping to the strains of martial music. Murder is murder, and somebody must answer. Somebody must explain the streams of blood that flowed in the Indian country in the summer of 1838. Somebody must explain the 4000 silent graves that mark the trail of the Cherokee to their exile. I wish I could forget it all, but the picture of 645 wagons lumbering over the frozen ground with their cargo of suffering humanity still lingers in my memory."

- Private John G. Burnett, who guided the Cherokee along the Trail of Tears, December 11th, 1890

President Andrew Jackson's original promise that the Cherokee would always remain in the East was easily broken. Chief Junaluska of the Cherokee helped General Jackson win the Battle of Horseshoe Bend. He supplied Jackson with five hundred troops and even allegedly saved

Jackson's life with his own tomahawk. But his service, support, and reinforcements were never repaid.

This penultimate betrayal set a precedent for the government's power over its people and the wards of the state. Before the Trail of Tears, unfair treaties were signed left and right; they were often forced onto the Native Americans to take their land, property, and more, all in the name of unity and typically some money and rights (if the agreement was upheld). But this cruel and hair-raising moment in history brings up questions about the foundation of the United States, the beliefs that it was built on, and whether or not they hold up today.

"We hold these truths to be self-evident, that all men are created equal, that they are endowed by their Creator with certain unalienable Rights, that among these are Life, Liberty, and the Pursuit of Happiness." These words echo throughout the United States, whether in school or in homes. This text shows the optimistic side of the United States of America: that all men were granted certain rights upon birth.

The Declaration of Independence also states, "That whenever any Form of Government becomes destructive of these ends, it is the Right of the People to alter or abolish it, and to institute New Government laying its foundation on such principles...as to them shall seem most likely to affect their Safety and Happiness." Who were the Founding Fathers thinking about when they drafted this text? What people crossed Thomas Jefferson's mind? Did John Adams wonder how these words would change the world?

Travel back to the Trail of Tears again. Think about the months leading up to their departure, the legal battles, and the cries that this was unjust and inhumane. It was an act that exiled an entire group of people to a territory far from their ancestral land. A forcible removal takes away the liberty and freedom of those who are made to suffer it. However, the Cherokee, although they had pledged allegiance to the flag and the United States of America, were not technically American citizens. As Supreme Court Justice John Marshall pointed out in the Indian Removal Act case, the relationship between the Cherokee and the US was more like a wardship than anything else.

The text itself, these sacred words, does not say, "We hold these truths to be self-evident, that all *American citizens* are created equal." The real question remains once all the extra has been sifted through: what does "men" truly mean? Does the term "men" not include the Cherokee citizens? The entirety of the Indigenous peoples who inhabited this land far before the European settlers ever discovered it?

The Trail of Tears could have been more aptly named the Trail of Death. The thousands they left buried along the trail in unmarked graves or with a talisman laid over the dirt left the Cherokee divided. It is believed that one in four Cherokee died along the Trail of Tears, and that is now considered to be a more conservative or modest estimate. An accurate toll may never be known.

Those who left their homes, survived the Trail of Tears, and arrived in Oklahoma were few and far between. Nevertheless, the land they arrived on was already taken. The Osage and Cherokees who had come before them had already set up shop on this land that was supposed to be theirs. Even the West could not belong to them.

Yet another promise was broken. Of course, the settlers likely didn't see things in this kind of light; they believed the land belonged to them as part of a greater destiny. The Cherokee land was excellent for raising cotton, and the continual need to produce more and earn more money was ever-present. The ability to relocate an entire group of people calls to mind the papal bull that Pope Alexander VI published. In it, he gave all Christians the ability to Christianize, civilize, and take over any savage Native peoples as long as they weren't Christian:

> "This assuredly ranks highest, that in our times especially the Catholic faith and the Christian religion be exalted and be everywhere increased and spread, that the health of souls be cared for and that barbarous nations be overthrown and brought to the faith itself."

- Pope Alexander VI, 1493

This was the precedent. This was the climate that the Europeans had created in the Americas. Religion gave the European Americans an excuse to push the Cherokee from their ancestral homeland. As long as the Native Americans were not Christian, then no sin was committed. But at this point in history, many Cherokee and other Native American tribes had converted to Christianity, even if only a minority.

Although the papal bull may have provided the security and comfort behind such a decision (it is likely that by the time the Trail of Tears took place, the average person probably wasn't aware of the bull), the true behemoth was the federal government. This was another turning point in

American history, a moment where people had to decide and realize how much power the federal government could have. The state of Georgia helped President Andrew Jackson, as well as Martin Van Buren, to expel the Cherokee. But the Indian Subsistence and Removal group allotted funds from the federal government, not from the local or state level.

What was seen as legal in the eyes of the federal government? According to the Constitution? Or the Declaration of Independence? And finally, how much power did the federal government truly have? Such an invasion would have been deemed impossible according to the Declaration of Independence. The sentiment that "all men are created equal" would surely disagree with such an action.

In the *American Indian Law Review*, published in 1991, author and attorney Mark Savage delves deep into the powers that Congress was granted by the Constitution in regard to the Native Americans, as well as the powers they used that were not necessarily completely legal. Savage's piece starts off with a fictionalized comparison of the Trail of Tears to a forced exile of all Vermonters, and in it, he purposefully emphasizes how strange, unbelievable, and unethical the Trail of Tears was. He later clarifies what powers Congress holds: "Congress has plenary power to legislate the form of government of Native Americans. Congress has plenary power to determine whether a 'tribe' does or does not exist and whether a Native American is or is not a citizen of it." Essentially, the US Congress has rights over what a Native American or a Native American tribe truly is. He further details the ways that the US has control over Native Americans, including property and their inability to form relationships and alliances outside of the US. He closes his statement by exploring the depth in which Congress controlled Native American life. Although citizenship was granted to all Native Americans, the rights of US citizens were not necessarily conferred to them. He finishes by saying, "Native Americans are not citizens in a constitutional sense."

As was established in several treaties after the Revolutionary War and the Cherokee War (Treaty of DeWitt's Corner, Treaty of Long Island Holston, etc.), Native Americans were only legally allowed to trade with US citizens. Any other foreign trade was illegal and punishable by federal law, not just tribal law. As can be seen above, the federal government (Congress) had control over the "rights and relations" of the Indigenous peoples of this country. Relations could include trade agreements, allegiances, and alliances formed in times of crises, economic hardships, or war.

Being a citizen of the United States of America does involve giving up certain liberties. Thomas Hobbes's social contract theory explains such sacrifices. In order to fully participate, be involved in, or belong to a society, one must sacrifice certain personal freedoms. He created this theory to delve deeper into the social need for society, as he claimed humans must live in a society in order to not descend into anarchy. The average sacrifices an American citizen makes on a daily basis could be as simple as buckling their seat belt, not driving ninety miles per hour in a neighborhood, or refraining from murder. In return, Americans are granted a country, laws that protect them and their families, and a sense of community.

Native Americans made sacrifices in order to be considered American citizens or even wards of the state. They pledged their allegiance to the flag, gave up their lucrative trade deals with the British, adopted a written language, converted to Christianity, and began farming, just to name a few. In *American Quarterly*, "Native Feminisms Engage American Studies" documents some of these sacrifices. "[Goeman] further contends that critical to such a nation-state form of governance is a relationship to land that sees land as fixed, enclosable, and as property. Within the context of claims against the state, Native peoples often must articulate their own land claims in a manner that recapitulates patriarchal and colonial constructions of land." The Native Americans had to give up their traditional relationship with the land in order to converse with the federal government, maintain the land they were on, and be understood. Despite their many sacrifices, both physical and spiritual, they were not granted the benefits that come with participating in such a society.

As Savage describes, the Native Americans were never true citizens or even guardians of the state. He later concludes that "the Constitution never conferred such power over Native Americans. Two hundred years of decisions by the Supreme Court and legislation by Congress and the President lack constitutional authority."

This expression of control, influence, and violence over the Native peoples—the Cherokee, Choctaw, and Seminoles in particular—created a precedent in US history on how the government can and may treat the *other*. This can be seen later on down the line in the treatment of the Chinese as they built the railroads, the Africans who were enslaved in the South for years, and the suffragette movement.

Hobbes's *Leviathan*, his most famous work, describes in detail his famous social contract theory. Here, he explains the three causes for invasion, war, or violence:

> "So that in the nature of man, we find three principal causes of quarrel:
>
> First, Competition;
>
> Secondly, Dissidence;
>
> Thirdly, Glory.
>
> The first, maketh men invade for Gain;
>
> The second, for Safety,
>
> And the third, for Reputation.
>
> The first use Violence, to make themselves Masters of other men's persons, wives, children and cattle;
>
> The second to defend them;
>
> The third, for trifles, as a word, a smile, a different opinion, and any other sign of undervalue, either direct in their Persons, or by reflexion in their Kindred, their Friends, their Nation, their Profession, or their Names."

If one was to use Hobbes's theory to explain the violence that was perpetrated on the Native Americans, one could easily find several, but perhaps competition was the biggest one of all. The Native Americans already inhabited this land and, in many ways, had a claim on it. The Europeans quickly fixed this issue by using Pope Alexander VI's papal bull as a reason to invade, conquer, and Christianize the so-called barbarous savages. The Americans sought a country that was free, splendid, and wealthy. The Cherokee stood in the way of their wealth.

Hobbes's theory supports their violence, as does the papal bull, but not necessarily the Constitution. The powers at be may have had historical documents to support them, but recent documents, findings, morality, and papers have proved them wrong. As mentioned before, Savage writes that the US had no "constitutional authority" to remove the Native Americans from their ancestral homeland. And so, America is left with a tarnished history of mistreating its citizens, non-citizens, refugees, and wards of the state. This is, by no means, unique to only the United States; perhaps it is a time for other countries to begin shining a light on the darker side of their past.

Chapter 8 – Unstable Times in Oklahoma

"I was hostile to the white man...We preferred hunting to a life of idleness on our reservations. At times we did not get enough to eat and we were not allowed to hunt. All we wanted was peace and to be let alone. Soldiers came...in the winter...and destroyed our villages. Then Long Hair (Custer) came...They said we massacred him, but he would have done the same to us. Our first impulse was to escape...but we were so hemmed in we had to fight. After that I lived in peace, but the government would not let me alone. I was no allowed to remain quiet. I was tired of fighting...They tried to confine me...and a soldier ran his bayonet into me. I have spoken."

- Crazy Horse, Chief of the Sioux

Those who survived the Trail of Tears were welcomed into Oklahoma with not-so-welcome arms. The previous Cherokee settlers and the new ones faced discrepancies in tradition, rituals, and boundaries, as they were forced to live together once again. The other tribes that occupied that territory, including the Osage, also caused territorial conflicts. However, as can be seen later in the 19th and 20th centuries, this land, according to the federal government, was never theirs to begin with.

Chief John Ross of the Cherokee was determined to keep his people united and the nation strong and continue their traditional practices. Chief John Ross managed to band together not only the survivors from the Trail of Tears but also the Cherokee who were already there, commonly called the "Old Settlers." Principal Chief Ross ratified the Cherokee Nation's

Constitution on September 6th, 1839. His efforts, along with those of several other Cherokee leaders and the community itself, allowed for a new building to house their Supreme Court, which was constructed in 1844. He even helped to establish and build their new capital city, Tahlequah. Chief John Ross didn't waste any time.

However, new problems soon arose. A storm was brewing in the United States, and the Cherokee were caught in the middle of it. Sectionalism was on the rise, and war soon broke out between the South and the North. Now known as the Civil War, this brother-against-brother violence was some of the bloodiest in the history of the nation.

Some of the wealthy Cherokee owned slaves. Similar to the South, only the elite few were able to own more than one or two enslaved persons. This part of Cherokee history is dark and unfortunate, just like the United States of America's history of slavery in the South. Many of the enslaved in the Cherokee tribe were chattel slaves, and the Cherokee had the most slaves of all the Five Civilized Tribes. Although many argue that the Cherokee had a gentler form of slavery, their constitution decreed that enslaved people had no right to vote, could not drink alcohol, own property, or marry a Cherokee. Though these rules were not enforced well or very often, they still existed.

Their new home was in Oklahoma, where the Confederacy reigned supreme. At first, Chief John Ross wanted to remain neutral and to stay out of the battle. They had just lost at least four thousand people, though some estimates range from eight thousand to nine thousand. They were rebuilding their society, learning to thrive in Oklahoma, and trying to build friendly relationships with their neighboring tribes. The Civil War changed everything for the Cherokee people. Their choices and actions were severely punished by the United States government, which ended up decimating their population. The dream of a new home where they would be left in peace was destroyed. There was no escaping this war, and the Cherokee were the tribe most affected by it.

In 1861, Chief John Ross finally signed a treaty that pledged their allegiance to the Confederate States of America. From 1861 to 1865, the Cherokee were swept up in a deadly and brutal war. At the time, the population of the Cherokee was at twenty-one thousand people. The twenty years between the Trail of Tears and the Civil War allowed them time to regroup and build up their society again.

Chief John Ross was soon rivaled by another member of their tribe: Stand Wattie. Brigadier-General Stand Watie became the second principal chief of the Cherokee, who were still under Chief John Ross. He would serve from 1862 to 1866. For context, Stand Watie was one of the few Cherokees who signed the Treaty of New Echota. Watie immediately sided with the Confederacy, splitting the tribe in half. He became the leader and general of the 1st Cherokee Mounted Rifles, which fought for the Confederacy. Fascinatingly, Stand Watie was the only Native American to ever be promoted to the role of general in the Civil War, Federal or Confederate.

However, this sudden shift in Cherokee policy had shadows in the past. Principal Chief John Ross never wanted to leave the East, while Stand Watie was one of the negotiators and signers of the Treaty of New Echota. Twenty years later, Chief John Ross wanted to stay neutral, while Watie sided with the Confederacy. Their disagreements were reflected within the tribe itself. Cherokee slaveholders wanted to support the Confederacy as well. The rest stayed with Chief John Ross, praying for neutrality, or they supported the Union.

In 1861, the Native American nations surrounding the Cherokee sided with the Confederacy. The federal government abandoned all Native American territory, withdrawing supplies and protection. Chief John Ross was forced to sign a deal with the Confederacy. In return for troops and men, the Confederacy would supply them with rations, protection, livestock, and tools. In addition, they would be able to keep their slaves. The Cherokee troops that fought for the Confederacy remained in Indian Territory. This deal, however necessary it may have been, could have been the greatest mistake Principal Chief John Ross ever made. Chief John Ross was stuck between a rock and a hard place. Seeking help, safety, and protection for his people, he reached out to the powers that be. In 1862, after Stand Watie sided with the Confederacy, Chief John Ross wrote the following to President Abraham Lincoln, praying that he would take his word instead of that of Watie's:

> "I...beg leave, very respectfully, to represent...that the relations which the Cherokee Nation sustains towards the United States have been defined by Treaties entered into between the Parties from time to time...Those Treaties were Treaties of Friendship and Alliance. The Cherokee Nation as the weaker party placing itself under the Protection of the United States and no other

Sovereign whatever, and the United States solemnly promising that Protection...That the Cherokee Nation maintained in good faith her relations towards the United States up to a late period and subsequent to the occurrence of the war between the Government and the Southern States of the Union and the withdrawal of all protection whatever by the Government...That in consequence of...the overwhelming pressure brought to bear upon them the Cherokees were forced for the preservation of their Country and their existence to negotiate a Treaty with the 'Confederate States'...That as soon as the Indian Expedition marched into the Country the Great Mass of the Cherokee People rallied spontaneously around the authorities of the United States and a large majority of their warriors are now engaged in fighting under the flag...What the Cherokee People now desire is ample Military Protection for life and property; a recognition by the Government of the obligations of existing Treaties and a willingness and determination to carry out the policy indicated by your Excellency of enforcing the Laws and extending to those who are loyal all the protection in your power."

This letter is a cry for help and support under the weight of the Confederate burden. Existing in the South put the Cherokee well within the Confederacy's reach. His people were endangered, injured, and even being killed by fellow Cherokee. Those who served under Stand Watie were known to kill the Cherokee who sided with the Union.

The Cherokee who had pledged themselves to the Confederacy called the other Cherokee "Pin" soldiers. The Union Pins fought against the Confederates brutally, and death plagued the Cherokee once again. Many Cherokee escaped Tahlequah to neutral states, only to return once the war ended to find their homes burned, orchards razed, and buildings demolished.

Then came the Battle of Pea Ridge. The year was 1862. The Cherokee had just sided with the Confederacy, the last of the Five Civilized Nations to join, and their troops were being asked to leave Indian Territory to fight offensively. Begrudgingly, they obeyed and traveled to northwestern Arkansas. Brigadier General Albert Pike's Indian Brigade was made up of almost three thousand men, one of the largest Native American armies in the Civil War. However, since Pike only managed to pay some of his men in a timely manner, they only had one-third of the men they were supposed to, so it largely consisted of Cherokee. Captain Otis Welch's Texas Cavalry Squadron was also able to join, increasing Pike's army by about one hundred men.

It should be noted that, according to historical documents and findings, the Five Civilized Tribes were largely untrained and unprepared for this war. Some were armed with shotguns and other such weaponry, but most of them were young and undisciplined. At first, the Confederate brigade succeeded. They overtook the Union at Foster's Farm. They celebrated, drinking and enjoying themselves, but a few snuck away. It was never proven or discovered who committed this war crime, but eight Union soldiers were scalped and mutilated. The blame was placed on Watie's men, but there were no eyewitnesses to the event. General Pike resigned in 1862 after the Battle of Pea Ridge, and he was later charged with allowing war crimes to occur.

However, after their initial victory at Pea Ridge, the Confederates soon hit a snag. On March 6th, the Confederates pushed forward to attack the Union stationed near Pea Ridge. Their general, Earl Van Dorn, ordered the supply trains to stay behind, hoping to make this a quick and smooth attack. He was wrong. The Union took down two Confederate generals, and since they had no supplies, the Confederates were soon defeated. The Union would hold Missouri for two years after this battle. The Confederacy suffered an estimated 2,500 casualties in this battle.

This Confederate, and therefore Cherokee, loss was just the tip of the iceberg. The Union was now back in Indian Territory. Come the summer of 1862, Chief John Ross was captured due to his previous allegiance with the Confederacy and taken to Washington. There, he spent the next four years advocating for Cherokee rights and begging the federal government to believe him when he said that the Cherokee were on the side of the Union and had been all along. In his absence, Stand Watie, his rival and a Confederate advocate, was elected as the new principal chief. Watie enacted a draft for all eighteen- to fifty-year-old Cherokee males. The in-house civil war for the Cherokee people remained. Watie ordered a raid in 1863 to burn down the homes of his political rivals and other buildings that represented their faction, including former Principal Chief John Ross's home.

After years of fighting, the Confederacy was defeated. General Stand Watie was the last to surrender, only doing so a full two months after General Robert E. Lee. The Cherokee lost six thousand lives in 1864, a full one-quarter of their population. Although the federal government ensured that all former Confederate Cherokees would be pardoned, their disloyalty was deemed to be more important, and such a pardoning never happened.

The Cherokee signed the Treaty of 1866 to close out the Civil War and hopefully usher in a new era of peace and unity. Chief John Ross died in Washington, DC, on August 1st, 1866. His attempts to unite the Cherokee and advocate for their rights as a people and as a tribe, as well as his rebuilding efforts, will go down in history.

In the midst of war, chaos, and strife, another event occurred that altered the future of the Cherokee people. In 1862, President Abraham Lincoln signed the Homestead Act, a provision that would redistribute all public land to private citizens. Almost 270 million acres were redistributed under the Homestead Act. Much of the West was undeveloped or unclaimed. But the Cherokee lived there, as did many other Native American nations. The sudden influx of homesteaders caused another round of encroachment on the Cherokees' land. Suddenly, there were major shifts in the terrain as well. It was no longer sustainable to continue the Cherokee way of life. Sustainable farming, harvesting, and agricultural practices were replaced by Western farming methods. Invasive plants overtook the land, and the buffalo population dwindled. The lands that the Cherokee were promised were eroding before their eyes.

These new settlers were wary of the Natives and their way of life. In 1883, Congress passed the Religious Crimes Code. This law banned all Native dancing, ceremonies, and the practice of medicine persons. Essentially, it banned their culture, decreeing it unlawful and a crime. Certain Native Americans and other officials were given the authority to stop these ceremonies by whatever means necessary. This could include violence, rationing of supplies to cause starvation or poverty, or even imprisonment. This land was not Native land, as it was meant to be. It was changing, and it was not changing in their favor.

The Native Americans were forced to hide their culture or practice in secret while fearing retribution. This became the norm for the Cherokee as well. Despite being the most "civilized" or "white" of the Five Nations, even they were too "native" for the settlers. Only four years passed before the next attack on the Native Americans. The Dawes Act of 1887 was created in order to further civilize Native Americans and push them into farming. The Dawes Act essentially redistributed all tribal lands to the heads of individual families. The thought behind it was that Native Americans could become more American if they owned land. Remember, Native Americans have had a very different relationship with the land they're on than the European settlers who came over.

However, these 160-acre plots were not given. They had to be bought. The families that could not afford to buy their own plot of land were left homeless and landless. Of course, the Cherokee were already at a financial disadvantage after the Trail of Tears and the Civil War. American settlers bought up the land eagerly, seeing as it was at a good price. By 1905, every piece of Native land in Oklahoma was made public.

Chitto Harjo, a Creek Indian, said it best:

> "Some citizens of the United States have title to land that was given to my fathers and my people by the government. If it was given to me, what right has the United States to take it from me without first asking my consent?"

According to the Library of Congress, "By 1932, the sale of both unclaimed land and allotted acreage resulted in the loss of two-thirds of the 138 million acres that Native Americans had held prior to the Dawes Act." The encroachment and cessions continued. The land that the Cherokee were promised in return for their brutal exile was taken from them. To be crystal clear, the land allotted for Native Americans and reservations went from 138 million acres to 48 million acres. The profits made off of selling unclaimed Native land were used by the local and federal government to create and build residential schools. These schools were yet another attempt to further civilize Native Americans and make them whiter.

At this point in time, Oklahoma was still not a state. In fact, Oklahoma would only become an official territory in 1890. As new settlers came in thanks to the Dawes Act, the cry for a recognized territory and even statehood was louder and more powerful than before. The federal government began making changes that would allow them to make Oklahoma a state, despite the Native American tribes that lived there under their own governance.

The Cherokee Strip land run in 1893 was an example of such land loss. After agreeing to sell their land to the government at a few dollars per acre, the soldiers organized a local land run to ensure a fair divide. Essentially, it was a finders-keepers situation. Almost six million acres were seized in the land run by over 100,000 participants. This land soon became a formal part of Oklahoma when it became a state, and it made up several counties.

In 1898, the Curtis Act was enacted. It abolished and dissolved all tribal courts and governance. Now, the only law was federal law. The Cherokee had developed a very American system of governance in the hopes of assimilating and winning favor with the Americans. Their Supreme Court, judicial branches, and Constitution were not enough to last in the era after the Homestead Act. In addition, the Curtis Act essentially ripped many Native Americans from their main source of income. The Curtis Act decreed that it was unlawful to claim royalties off of natural resources (such as minerals, oils, lumber, etc.) or property on land belonging to a Native American tribe. The royalties that should belong to the property owners or leasers were to be sent to the Treasury of the United States.

The Cherokee were now unable to govern their own people or make money off of their land, which was a regular source of income, as they could rent fields for cattle grazing. Their money, if it was made in a way deemed appropriate by the Curtis Act, went straight to the US Treasury. This so-called promised land was nothing more than a hoax. So long as there was land to farm, resources to mine, or water to source, their given land would never be theirs.

Poverty soon befell the Cherokee. Those who could afford to buy back their land struggled to survive off of it. And those who couldn't? It was hopeless from the beginning. In 1882, the Indian Rights Association was founded in Philadelphia. Although this was states away from Oklahoma, their influence was felt throughout the whole country. The name may sound promising, but the true beliefs of this group went against Native American cultures and customs. Floyd O'Neil, who grew up on the Ute Reservation in Utah, described the Indians Rights Association's superstitions and ideals in his novel, *The Indian New Deal: An Overview*: "[Their beliefs] were (1) that farming was superior to hunting, (2) that alcohol was evil, (3) that idleness was the ultimate evil, and (4) that Christianity was a magic elixir that would change people and, therefore, the Christian religion should take a very strong position in American life and assume a strong proselytizing stance." Native American tribes in the West, though, tended to rely more on a nomadic lifestyle than an agricultural one. But their opinions didn't stop there. "Essential to this view of Christianity was the idea that the existence of tribes was evil.

Therefore, only as individual men who loved property and sought it could Indians ever really be assimilated successfully into the general population."

However, according to O'Neil, "By the year 1920, the people of the United States had a change of heart about Indian life. This change was caused, in part, by a back-to-nature movement. The founding of national parks, where people could go to be alone and commune with nature, reminded many Americans of the lives that Indian people had been forced to give up." Finally, the rhetoric surrounding the Indigenous peoples of this country was starting to change. The idea of the "vanishing American" was now vanishing. The Native Americans were essentially making a comeback.

One of the instigators of this change was the Meriam Report. This report was requested by Secretary of the Interior Hubert Work, and it was performed by the Institute for Government Research, led by Lewis Meriam—hence the name of the Meriam Report. They collected data in the field for a little under one year before preparing it all in this report. The report, which was published on February 21st, 1928, revealed just how terrible the Native Americans' living conditions were. The first sentence of the general summary of the Meriam Report is as follows: "An overwhelming majority of the Indians are poor, even extremely poor, and they are not adjusted to the economic and social system of the dominant white civilization." The report continues to describe the living conditions, their health, the living facilities, and the day-to-day life of the Native Americans. Their health, generally speaking, was very bad. For instance, the death and infant mortality rates were high, and tuberculosis was a constant problem. In the 20th and 21st centuries, the greatest sign of technological and medical advancements was the decrease in infant mortality rates. However, the exact opposite occurred for the Native Americans.

In addition, the spread of these diseases, such as tuberculosis and trachoma (a communicable disease that causes blindness), was made possible due to the living facilities of the Native Americans. They lived in crowded conditions, which made it easy for transmissible diseases to spread, especially since there was no way to isolate an infected person. As we have all learned in 2020 onward, the need for separate rooms when it comes to quarantining the infected is an absolute must, especially when diseases like tuberculosis and trachoma are prevalent.

Very few Native Americans had sufficient sanitary facilities or even access to water. Many had to walk far distances to retrieve pails of water, only to carry it right back. Their economic conditions were just as poor:

> "The income of the typical Indian family is low and the earned income extremely low. From the standpoint of the white man the typical Indian is not industrious, nor is he an effective worker when he does work...He generally ekes out an existence through unearned income from leases of his land, the sale of land, per capita payments from tribal funds, or in exceptional cases through rations given him by the government. The number of Indians who are supporting themselves through their own efforts, according to what a white man would regard as the minimum standard of health and decency, is extremely small."

According to this report, the Native Americans who were lucky enough to be well-off by their standards barely met the "minimum standard of health and decency." The report then delves into the agricultural conditions since many of the Native Americans worked on farms or in agriculture. It states that the land on which they toiled was incredibly difficult, nearing impossible to grow crops on. Since the Native Americans bought their own land back from the government, many chose it based on location or resources. Few were able to grow a reasonable amount on the land, and "many of [the Native Americans] are living on lands from which a trained and experienced white man could scarcely wrest a reasonable living." Even with years of farming experience, money, and irrigation systems, the land was still difficult to grow on.

Even the author of the Meriam Report admitted that even the richer Native Americans who had a sizable plot of land or land that was fit for farming were unable to make decent money off of it because of their ignorance. The Oklahoma land, in certain areas, was notably dry, hot, and difficult to grow crops on. Some turned to cattle herding and renting out land for grazing in order to make ends meet.

There are a few sentences that truly stand out in the Meriam Report. The first section comes from "Suffering and Discontent": "The Indian is like the white man in his affection for his children and feels keenly the sickness and the loss of his offspring." This sentence exemplifies the utter distance between the white man and the Native American and the ignorant thinking of white men. Here, it's practically implied that a Native American man is not even human. This ignorance made it easier to push the Native Americans off of their land and slowly erase their culture.

The second and final example comes from "The Causes of Poverty":

> "The economic basis of the primitive culture of the Indians has been largely destroyed by the encroachment of white civilization. The Indians can no longer make a living as they did in the past by hunting, fishing, gathering wild products, and the extremely limited practice of primitive agriculture. The social system that evolved from their past economic life is ill suited to the conditions that now confront them, notably in the matter of the division of labor between the men and women. They are by no means yet adjusted to the new economic and social conditions that confront them."

As mentioned above, the Native Americans, Cherokee included, were not Eurocentric farmers by nature. Their toil with the land and nature came through symbiotic hunting, fishing, and harvesting. Their inability to adapt and evolve to the European way of life was because of their lack of resources, education, and kinship. The Meriam Report enlightened the federal government, as well as many of the ordinary people, on the plight and unjust treatment of the Native Americans. Change was on the horizon.

After decades of impoverished living, unjust acts and deals, and harsh conditions, President Franklin Roosevelt passed the Indian Reorganization Act. The year was 1934, and this act decreed that tribal land could no longer be sold and that some of the original tribal lands were to be returned to the true owners. Roosevelt created the Indian Reorganization Act "to conserve and develop Indian lands and resources," grant Native Americans the right to establish businesses, create a credit system, and provide vocational educational opportunities, to name a few.

Roosevelt made up for the previous wrongdoings by reversing them. The successes and failures from this act both proved him right and wrong, but at last, the Native Americans had someone looking out for their best interests. The Indian Reorganization Act also gave Native Americans some of their old tribal rights; they could employ legal counsel, prevent the sale or lease of tribal lands, and negotiate with federal, state, and local governments. This section redefines tribal governments and the rights allotted to specific individuals, tribal councils, and the government as a whole.

However, the Indian Reorganization Act, also called the IRA and the Indian New Deal, was not accepted by everyone. When it came down to it, the individual tribes were allowed to vote on whether or not to pass the IRA within their own tribe. Some said yes, while some said no. A few historians claim that the tribes who refused the IRA to take effect were manipulated or persuaded by white men who wanted to buy their land. Others had justifiable reasons.

John Collier, an Indian commissioner, was one of the main leaders and heralds of the Indian Reorganization Act. His work on this project pushed it across the finish line. But just like the Indian New Deal, he is not remembered all too fondly. Of course, there's contentious debate on the subject of these two hot topics. However, it's important to recognize that there are always two sides to every story.

American historian Wilcomb Washburn, a contributor to *The IRA Record and John Collier*, speaks openly about his feelings for John Collier. They are mostly positive, and he cites his encounters with him and his opinions about the Native American state of affairs at that time. He writes,

> "I would like to elaborate on the apparent contradiction between Collier's approach to Indian culture and religion on the one hand and his approach to economics and politics on the other. There is no real contradiction. The alternative to involving tribes in the context of the American political system was not that they would remain independent nation-states. It was that they would be extinguished entirely. I do not think there would be a single Indian tribe in existence today if it had not been for John Collier and the Indian Reorganization Act."

Washburn's opinion is clear; even if he may not agree with some of the policies, programs, or structures of the Indian Reorganization Act, he recognizes that there was a need for action, lest the Native Americans would face extinction. Washburn even defends John Collier in his statement: "Most of the critiques of John Collier have simply overlooked this reality. They judge his work against an ideal standard, on the one hand, or against his character, on the other hand."

One ardent disputant of Collier's IRA was Rupert Costo, one of the founders of the American Indian Historical Society. Costo, a member of the Cahuilla tribe, spread his opinions about the IRA and John Collier far and wide, so much so that he's one of the main voices of the opposition. Tim Giago, a Native American journalist at the *Native Sun News*, recorded Costo's thoughts on the IRA at the fiftieth anniversary of the

Indian New Deal conference in 1983.

> "The IRA was the last great drive to assimilate the American Indian. It was also a program to colonize the tribes. All else had failed to liberate the Indians from their land: genocide, treaty-making and treaty-breaking, sub-standard education, disruption of Indian religion and culture, and the last and most oppressive of such measures, the Dawes Allotment Act. Assimilation into the dominant society, if by assimilation we mean the adoption of certain technologies and techniques, had already been underway for some hundred years. After all, the Indians were not and are not fools; we are always ready to improve our condition. But assimilation, meaning fading into the general society with a complete loss of our identity and our culture, was another thing entirely, and we had fought against this from the first coming of the white man."

Despite the new economic boons, the programs intended to help Native Americans, and the return of some of their land, Rupert Costo viewed the Indian New Deal in a completely negative light. In Costo's eyes, the Indian Reorganization Act was simply another way to force the Native Americans to assimilate and further blend into American society. This sneakier way of forced assimilation caught them by surprise, and so some signed on, believing it was for the best. Those who didn't vote for the IRA had plenty of good reasons not to. The federal government tended to ration grant and program money, and they would not dole out enough for Native American causes. In addition, this program was white-founded and white-funded. There was a lot of mistrust in the federal government and system. The generational trauma and wounds that were passed down were not easily erased. Great-grandparents and infants alike carried scars that were inflicted by Americans, whether knowingly or unknowingly.

Chapter 9 – A Brief History of Residential Schools

"The unique events of two generations, culminating in a crisis of political necessity, catapulted this man into a position of historic importance. He rode to office on the wings of those events. He stood on the shoulders of many who had gone before and made himself into a figure of national importance and influence. But John Collier betrayed us. His autocratic administration and repressive administration damned him before the Indians, creating that fault line in historic estimates of Collier and his works which finally cast him from his seat at the side of the white man's Jesus Christ, where some historians have mistakenly placed him."

- Rupert Costo, Cahuilla

So, what now? Although Costo may not have been entirely correct in his statements about the IRA and John Collier, he was right about one thing: the Native Americans were forced to assimilate even further. Sadly, the residential school system began several decades before the IRA; however, the IRA did aim to improve education. In this case, the improved education meant more residential schools, so Native Americans could better themselves and contribute to society successfully, productively, and respectfully.

However, in order to do so, sacrifices must be made. At least, Captain Richard Pratt, the founder of the Carlisle Indian Industrial School in Pennsylvania, which opened in 1879, believed so. He is most famous for saying, "Kill the Indian to save the man." Soon, this mantra became a part of a well-developed system, a method of erasing culture by civilizing children in boarding schools with little to no contact with their families. These schools were built on fear, forcing kids to change their appearance and abandon their native language and customs, all in favor of appearing more "civilized."

The first residential schools were built in 1819 after the Civilization Fund Act was passed. Oftentimes, children were forcibly removed from their homes and taken away to these boarding schools. In modern-day terms, this was literally kidnapping. Children were forced to cut their hair. Long hair was a well-known staple of Native American culture, as it tied them back to their tribe, family, and culture. Barbie Stensgar, founder of Sister Sky—a natural alternative Native American-founded company—recounted how her grandfather was forced to cut his hair when he attended boarding school. "When I was about five years old, my grandfather first told me about being forced to cut his hair when he was carted off to boarding school...Eventually, he told me his hair was cut...to strip him of his culture and identity." In many Native American tribes, it was taught to never cut one's hair unless they had experienced an incredibly significant loss, such as a death in the family. Even then, their hair was disposed of in a proper way, burnt with sweetgrass and sage, not just thrown away.

These schools were essentially cultural genocide. Some kids were only two years old when they were carted away to a boarding school. According to the Meriam Report, "More Indian children are now in public schools maintained by the state or local governments than in special Indian schools maintained by the nation." The Meriam Report was published in the late 1920s, over one hundred years after the first residential school was built. Despite being schools of the state and federal governments, their funding, supplies, and dormitories were inadequate for children of any age. Many suffered from disease and illness due to poor diets and crowded dormitories. The buildings themselves had lavatories that were insufficient for the number of people there, as well as an unreasonably small supply of towels and soap.

Sadly, children were often forced to work as laborers for the school in order to keep the buildings up and running. In the "Formal Education of Indian Children" section, the Meriam Report claims that, "The question may very properly be raised as to whether much of the work of Indian children in boarding schools would not be prohibited in many states by the child labor laws." The schools that were ripping these children away from their families, erasing their cultural heritage, and forcing them to abandon their languages also made them work to maintain the institution itself. But it didn't stop there. Many children were beaten and whipped. If they protested having their hair cut, were caught speaking their native language, or committed any other alleged crime, they were often punished with violence.

The Cherokee Boarding School began enrolling—or kidnapping—students in 1881. It was a Quaker school, and it, like many other residential schools, took a Christian perspective when it came to education. However, the Quaker version of this school only lasted until June 30th, 1892, when it was promptly shut down. The reason for this was the United States was beginning to shy away from missionary-style schools in favor of more federal-mandated and -operated institutions. According to Karen French Owl, one of the authors of *The Cherokee Perspective*, "Students were punished for speaking Cherokee; some had their mouths washed with soap for speaking Cherokee and some were beaten." The students who boarded at these schools were forced to wear military-style uniforms. Those who were lucky enough to remain at home and only attend during the day were permitted to wear their normal attire.

Despite all of this madness, some Cherokee educators truly believed that this was the best way to help Native Americans rise in the ranks of society. An anonymous Cherokee educator wrote out the "Education Needs of the American Indians" with eight rules or ideals to stand by. His concluding remarks were as follows:

> "I can state freely, without reservation (no pun intended), that the American Indian can only better himself by learning to understand the white man's way of life; learn to stand on his own two feet...stop standing around waiting for someone to offer him a better life, free of charge and requiring little or no effort on his part; stop feeling that because his ancestors were mistreated the world owes him a living. In other words, if the American Indian is ever to reach goals/levels in comparison to his white counterparts, he must accept the fact that his counterparts have risen to their status by dedication and hard work, not by feeling sorry for themselves and that no one gave it to them."

These words came from a man who was raised on a reservation and attended such a school. Perhaps he recognized that in order to rise to the top of white society at that time, one must become as white as possible. However, recent revelations and firsthand testimonies have shifted the public perspective on residential schools. At first, they may have been thought of as a gift from the federal government to the Native Americans, a way to help them contribute to society. Then, they were seen as a necessary evil. Today, many see them as being simply evil.

Dwight Mission, one of the Cherokee residential schools, was just purchased by the Cherokee Nation in 2021. Principal Chief Chuck Hoskin Jr. decided to purchase the iconic mansion in order to preserve historical accuracy and integrity, as well as to repurpose it to better serve the Cherokee people. Chief Hoskin, the eighteenth elected principal chief of the Cherokee, wrote a brief article detailing the history of this building, as well as its significance in Cherokee society. It was originally built in 1820 in Arkansas, which was before the previously settled Cherokee were forced to move into what is now Oklahoma. The school reopened in 1830 and taught students for over one hundred years before eventually closing in 1948. It has been used by the Presbyterian Church as a site for camps and conferences.

Dwight Mission proves that not all residential schools were dangerous. Though these schools were few and far between, some were created by the Native Americans for other Native Americans. However, even Dwight Mission was touched by tragedy. A great fire tore through the campus and took several young lives, potentially causing its closure. However, Dwight Mission was just one of eighty residential schools for the Cherokee Nation. Principal Chief Hoskin touches on the violent history of residential schools:

> "Indian missions, like Indian residential schools established by the Department of the Interior, provided Indian children with boarding, education and exposure to religion designed to assimilate the children into mainstream culture. This assimilation came at a steep price to Native people across the United States, a price we are still paying today in terms of the erosion of indigenous languages, cultures, lifeways, and the very loss of life among some students."

His words are diplomatic, but they ring true. US Secretary of the Interior Deb Haaland, the first Native American to serve as a cabinet secretary, says things a little more bluntly.

"In most instances, Indigenous parents could not visit their children at these schools. Many students endured routine injury and abuse. Some perished and were interred in unmarked graves. Survivors of the traumas of boarding school policies carried their memories into adulthood as they became the aunts and uncles, parents, and grandparents to subsequent generations. The loss of those who did not return left an enduring need in their families for answers that, in many cases, were never provided...The assimilationist policies of the past are contrary to the doctrine of trust responsibility, under which the Federal Government must promote Tribal self-governance and cultural integrity. Nevertheless, the legacy of Indian boarding schools remains, manifesting itself in Indigenous communities through intergenerational trauma, cycles of violence and abuse, disappearance, premature deaths, and other undocumented bodily and mental impacts."

According to the National Native American Boarding School Healing Coalition, by 1900, twenty thousand children attended boarding schools. By 1926, over sixty thousand children were enrolled, meaning over 80 percent of Indigenous children were students in federal government or religious residential schools. There were 367 boarding schools in the United States spread out in 29 states.

Time and a new perspective have illuminated the wrongful past of the Native Americans. The history of residential schools in the United States of America, as well as Canada, is just now being uncovered. Recent revelations and discoveries have led to widespread investigations into the lives of those who lived in these schools, as well as their unexplained deaths. This process will not be over quickly, however. Children were enrolled in residential schools all across the country for over 150 years.

However, the United States was not alone in its treatment of its Indigenous children. Canada built and hosted several residential schools for Aboriginal children, and they were all required to attend if they were below the age of sixteen. The recent discovery of a mass grave at a Canadian residential school ignited the movement and pushed officials to investigate all of the schools.

Garnet Angeconeb, an Indigenous man, described his experience in a Canadian residential school through a series of videos posted online. His mission is as follows: "Through hope there is healing. Through healing there is restoration. Through restoration there is forgiveness. Through forgiveness there is peace." A former Pelican Indian Residential School student, Angeconeb attended from 1963 to 1969, beginning at age seven. In his few years there, he experienced several forms of abuse at the hands of his classmates and teachers.

Lydia Ross attended a Canadian residential school as well and detailed her experiences:

> "My name was Lydia, but in the school I was, I didn't have a name, I had numbers. I had number 51, number 44, number 32, number 16, number 11, and then finally number one when I was just about coming to high school. So, I wasn't, I didn't have a name, I had numbers."

Denise Lajimodiere, Ojibwe author and citizen of the Turtle Mountain Band of Chippewa in North Dakota, told the story of her parent's time in a residential school to Minnesota Public Radio.

> "Mama was made to kneel on a broomstick for not speaking English, locked in closets for not speaking English. They would pee their pants and then the nuns would take them out [of the closet] and beat them for peeing their pants...Papa was beaten with a belt. He saw one of his fellow students die from a beating at the school...Papa said, "I just couldn't learn that language," so they put lye soap in his mouth and the kids would get blisters...My father never spoke Cree again; that was completely beaten out of him."

Lajimodiere took her parents' stories to heart when she first heard them. They explained the dysfunction in their family system, the drinking, the abuse, and the neglect. She decided to take her journey one step further by interviewing many of the elderly Natives in her community, asking them to release the secrets and stories they'd been holding close to their chest for so long. Her book, *Stringing Rosaries*, details these stories in full. Her mission is as follows: "I want the world to know that part of why we are the way we are. With high alcoholism, high diabetes and a lot of other health issues, one of the overarching reasons is the boarding school era." The trauma that has now been passed down from generation to generation has distinctly and severely affected the up-and-coming.

The Genoa US Indian Industrial School in Genoa, Nebraska, is home to a mass grave of at least 102 Indigenous children. However, the true death toll is most likely much higher. According to Richard Luscombe of *The Guardian*, "some of the students, aged four to 22, died in accidents, by drowning or by shooting and in one case reportedly after being hit by a freight train. But most died from disease. Tuberculosis and pneumonia were rife in the federal Indian school system." The proof is in the pudding. The Meriam Report discovered high cases of tuberculosis, pneumonia, and trachoma throughout these schools. And they only investigated around ninety schools. There were almost four hundred residential schools in the United States. The current investigations are sure to uncover more mass graves, more covered-up tragedies, and more atrocities that we wish we could forget.

How did it come to this? How did North America turn to committing cultural genocide on children as a way to assimilate the Native Americans and Aboriginal populations? Tracing the timeline leads to a deep misunderstanding of Indigenous culture, not to mention a deep disrespect. The fear of difference, of not having claim to this land, and of change not only gave Americans and Canadians the "right" to create these schools but also justified it. This unnatural fear of the other can be seen in other facets of American history, most ardently through the treatment of African Americans. Captain Richard Pratt, the founder of the Carlisle Indian Industrial School in Pennsylvania, compared the Native American residential schools to servitude on US soil. He considered slavery, though terrible in essence, to be a blessing for the Africans who came to the country's shores. According to Pratt, slavery helped the Africans become American citizens, though this was only possible once they had fully assimilated, adopted Christianity, and accepted the biblical God as the one true power. Here, he compares the necessities of slavery to residential schools:

> "As we have taken into our national family seven millions of Negroes, and as we receive foreigners at the rate of more than five hundred thousand a year, and assimilate them, it would seem that the time may have arrived when we can very properly make at least the attempt to assimilate our two hundred and fifty thousand Indians, using the proven potent line, and see if that will not end this vexed question and remove them from public attention, where they occupy so much more space than they are entitled to either by numbers or worth."

When the Indian Removal Act was enacted in the 1830s, Supreme Court Justice John Marshall described the relationship between the United States federal government and the Native American nations as a wardship. Here, it seems as though that thought pattern had completely reversed. This transition is marked by the sudden force of assimilation. Pratt describes his ideas surrounding the differences between Indian schools versus missionary/federal residential schools as well. He claims that Native American schools only produce Natives, not Americans. They were taught to exist within the nation or tribe but not the country as a whole. Captain Pratt also says, "[The Indian schools] formulate the notion that the government owes them a living and vast sums of money" and "[leaves] them in their chronic condition of helplessness." Pratt follows this up by saying that those who attended Native American schools were not fit to compete with their white counterparts, claiming they were unequal in education. He believed that bringing Native Americans to a residential school would force them to assimilate and become Americans. This shows a gross misunderstanding of the Native American cultures and tribal systems as a whole. The notion of Christian and American superiority is greatly inflated here, backed up as always by Pope Alexander IV's papal bull. Pratt's negative analysis of the Native Americans' wish to remain by or near their tribe, whether that be culturally or professional, is ludicrous. Although his public school systems were designed to make all the races unified and equal, in truth, those who attended residential schools and were "civilized" were rarely accepted into American society. And those who were did not receive the same treatment, same opportunities, or similar status to their white counterparts.

In fact, those who attended residential schools were stripped of their culture and heritage (some successfully, some not so much) so much so that some felt as if they neither belonged in their tribe or in white society. Sometimes those who assimilated were not welcomed back into their tribes with open arms. Stuck in the purgatory of ambiguous identity, their mistrust of the federal government only grew. How could these schools be created to unify the races and teach kids to respect their federal government when, in practice, they did the exact opposite?

Let us never forget the opening words of Captain Richard Pratt's speech in 1892, words that will haunt the United States for the rest of history.

> "A great general has said that the only good Indian is a dead one, and that high sanction of his destruction has been an enormous factor in promoting Indian massacres. In a sense, I agree with the

sentiment, but only in this: that all the Indian there is in the race should be dead. Kill the Indian in him, and save the man."

Chapter 10 – The Cherokee in the 20th and 21st Centuries

"Nothing saves the day so much as a good word. And nothing has been misused as often. There is power in a word, whether we read it, speak it or hear it. And we command and are commanded by the word. We scatter, we call forth, and we comfort. Words are tools, weapons, both good and bad medicine-but very beautiful when used lovingly. The word, or ka ne tsv in Cherokee, is power to help heal, or make sick people sicker by negative talk around them. The word gives confidence when it builds rather than destroys. Relationships have been shattered beyond by a runaway mouth. Prosperity has been dissolved by talking lack. Until we listen to our own voices and how we talk, we would never guess how we use our words."

- Joyce Sequichie Hifler

They survived the European encroachment. They survived the Seven Years' War. They survived the Revolutionary War, the Cherokee War, and the Civil War. They survived the Trail of Tears, the residential school system, and the decimation of their tribal governments. Wilma Mankiller, the first female principal chief of the Cherokee Nation, said it best:

> "We are a revitalized tribe. After every major upheaval, we have been able to gather together as a people to rebuild a community and a government. Individually and collectively, Cherokee people possess an extraordinary ability to face down adversity and continue moving forward. We are able to do that because our

culture, though certainly diminished, has sustained us since time immemorial. This Cherokee culture is a well-kept secret."

We have now arrived to the events of the 20th century. The civil rights movement is on the cusp of emergence. The Cherokee Nation rules over the Eastern Band of Cherokee Indians, the Cherokee Nation of Oklahoma, and the United Keetoowah Band of Cherokees. Cultural movements are taking place across the nation: the rights of women, the rights of African Americans, and the rights of Native Americans.

Before the Indian Reorganization Act, the only way to legally identify and belong to the Cherokee or any other Native American tribe was through one's blood quantum. The blood quantum is a way of measuring ancestry and identifying how much Native blood runs in a person's veins. For years, it was used as a way to further divide the Native American tribes. Not everyone had the necessary amount of blood needed to remain in the tribe. Thus, they were stripped of their federal and tribal rights as a Native American. The blood quantum was also used to further the Dawes Act and the entire allotment movement.

Most tribal enrollments required the subject to have at least one-fourth Native blood. Although the Cherokee Nation does not require this, the United Keetoowah Band of Cherokee does. Once an Indigenous person qualifies under the blood quantum policy, they are given a Certificate of Degree of Indian Blood, or a CDIB, stating their blood percentages and which tribe they belong to. However, this is incredibly problematic in modern-day standards, not only from a humanitarian standpoint but also a scientific one. Elizabeth Rule, a specialist in Native American studies and member of the Chickasaw Nation, was interviewed by **NPR** about the blood quantum policies and their effects on Native nations: "Blood quantum emerged as a way to measure 'Indian-ness' through a construct of race. So that over time, Indians would literally breed themselves out and rid the federal government of their legal duties to uphold treaty obligations."

But as can be seen throughout history, intermarriage does occur, and Native blood, according to the blood quantum, will dwindle, effectively eliminating all Indigenous peoples. However, if we view Native Americans as members of a culture or family, instead of tied down to the blood in their veins, the real truth emerges.

Freedmen (those who had once been slaves) were often a part of Native tribes due to their early enslavement. However, under the blood quantum, they do not federally qualify as citizens of these tribes. When the Dawes Rolls were taken, several freedmen who were members of the Cherokee tribe before were not included in the list. This has caused some disparities in the ancestry rolls in deciding who is actually Cherokee and who is not. This history has continued into the 21st century, with the Cherokee Nation stripping many freedmen of their Cherokee ancestry and removing them from the tribe. This highly controversial decision faced much backlash when it was announced in the 2010s.

Once the Indian Reorganization Act was passed, voted on, and implemented, individual tribes had the option to continue using the blood quantum or not. Interestingly enough, many tribes still use the blood quantum as a way to measure Native-ness, including the Navajo Nation and some Chippewa bands. The Cherokee Nation does not have a blood quantum requirement for citizenship. In fact, many citizens of the Cherokee Nation have blood that is below the minimum blood quantum (one-fourth). However, they use the Dawes Rolls to look at who was deemed a citizen way back when. Although some may only have 1/256 Cherokee blood, using the Dawes Rolls excludes many Cherokee citizens, freedmen included, from tribal benefits and being a part of the community. As well, the Cherokee Nation allows for dual citizenship. The Eastern Band of Cherokees does have a blood quantum requirement, and the United Keetoowah Band of Cherokee requires at least one-fourth.

Although the Indian Reorganization Act of 1934 granted more rights to the Cherokee people and Native Americans as a whole, they were still regarded as lesser when compared to American citizens overall. Of course, the Snyder Act of 1924 gave all Native Americans full US citizenship (those born within United States boundaries), but in practice, things were a little trickier. Due to the complicated and difficult relationship between the state government and federal government, Native Americans, especially those in the western states, were still unable to vote in federal elections. Since states decided who got to vote, the Snyder Act did not fully extend the rights of an American citizen onto Indigenous peoples. There was also the issue of poll taxes and literacy tests, which further discouraged Native Americans from voting.

According to a study from 2000, Native American households had eight cents for every dollar that the average white American household had. And sadly, this gap in wealth and means has only increased as the years have gone by. In addition, as of 2020, there were 4.7 million Native

Americans who could register to vote; however, only 66 percent of them are registered. Of course, there are several reasons for this, such as,

> "(1) geographical isolation; (2) physical and natural barriers; (3) poorly maintained or non-existent roads; (4) distance and limited hours of government offices; (5) technological barriers and the digital divide; (6) low levels of educational attainment; (7) depressed socio-economic conditions; (8) homelessness and housing insecurity; (9) non-traditional mailing addresses...;(10) lack of funding for elections; (11) and discrimination against Native Americans."

- NARF Comprehensive Field Hearing Report 2020

Though, in many ways, it is ironic that the Native Americans, just like African Americans and women, were denied voting rights for so long when the government's mission—or, at least, Captain Pratt's mission—was to assimilate them. What can be more American than voting? A democracy is nothing without a way to hear the voices of the people, and voting has and always will be one of the most sacred rights.

Although the United States is a first-world country, there are varying levels of wealth and poverty within its borders. According to the NARF Comprehensive Field Hearing Report completed in 2020, "Native peoples have the highest poverty rate of any population group, 26.6 percent, which is nearly double the poverty rate of the nation as a whole. The poverty rate was even higher on federally recognized Indian reservations." This high poverty rate leads to even higher levels of homelessness amongst self-identifying Native American individuals as well.

Those who can barely afford to live cannot afford to take care of themselves either. Healthy food can be quite costly, and those who live on reservations are often subjected to much higher costs. A 2016 brief report titled "Causes of Mortality in Cherokee Nation," published by Cherokee Nation Public Health, discovered that the leading causes of death were heart disease, cancer, diabetes, lower respiratory disease, stroke, and suicide. Suicide is the most prevalent among Cherokee citizens from five to forty-four years of age. This study concluded with:

> "Cigarette smoking, lack of physical activity, and poor nutrition are important modifiable risk factors in many of the leading causes of death. However, the impact of mental health is poorly measured and described in our communities. Data on behavioral health issues are difficult to gather and interpret due to the sensitive

nature and cultural barriers encountered. This problem is not unique to Cherokee Nation, but is an issue nation-wide."

Many of these causes of death can also be attributed to the high alcoholism rates in Native American communities. The National Survey on Drug Use and Health states that "nearly 9.2% of Native Americans ages 12 and older were current heavy alcohol users, the highest rate of any ethnic group." Native American reservations are not able to set their own minimum age requirement, but they do have the option to ban alcohol from the reservation. On top of that, Native Americans also have the highest rates of death from overdoses, as well as some of the highest rates of fetal alcohol spectrum disorders (FASD).

Now, this doesn't paint a very pretty picture. But imagine having to endure hundreds of years of genocide, generational trauma, and forced exile. Think about the thousands of deaths, buildings burned, homes pillaged, and friends and family raped. Imagine watching your child be sent to a residential school, only to return home with a shaved head and fear in their eyes. Without equal opportunity, acceptance, and respect, the Indigenous peoples of the United States have struggled for a foothold in American society.

However, their culture and faith have remained strong. Wilma Mankiller, the first female principal chief of the Cherokee Nation, rose from the bottom up. Before the settlers arrived, Cherokee women were considered equal to men. Children were only related to the maternal line, so everything stemmed from the mother. Women acted as gatherers and horticulturalists while the men hunted. They also had an equal voice in government. When the Europeans came and assimilation occurred, the Cherokee way of life and government began to resemble the Eurocentric way, where women were considered less than men.

This history makes Chief Mankiller's election even more powerful. Chief Mankiller and her eleven siblings were raised in a rural home without any modern amenities, like indoor plumbing or electricity. Her family moved to San Francisco as a victim of the Bureau of Indian Affairs' relocation promises, but she returned to the Cherokee Nation with the heart of an activist. She served as chief for ten years and brought about great change. While in office, the population of the Cherokee Nation doubled in size—68,000 to 170,000—and was a recipient of the Presidential Medal of Freedom.

She rebuilt the relationship between the Cherokee Nation and the US government. Chief Mankiller "revitalized the Nation's tribal government, and advocated relentlessly for improved education, healthcare, and housing services." During her tenure, infant mortality rates declined, and education climbed.

Her power and presence as both a Cherokee woman and leader in a time of great hardship will forever be remembered. If we move forward in time to the 21st century, we can see that a great Indigenous rights movement is taking place. The Land Back movement advocates for realizing what Native land each American city stands on today. The Cherokee Nation will raise its minimum wage to fifteen dollars an hour by 2025. Native Americans are finally being recognized for their relationship with the land and are now being asked for agricultural and environmental advice.

The past is bleak and grim. Frankly, it can hurt to look at. But without the knowledge of yesterday, we will never forge ahead to build a better tomorrow. Here's some advice Chief Mankiller once gave to an old friend:

> "Be the buffalo. Wilma Mankiller, the first female principal chief of the Cherokee Nation, once told me how the cow runs away from the storm while the buffalo charges directly toward it - and gets through it quicker. Whenever I'm confronted with a tough challenge, I do not prolong the torment. I become the buffalo."

Conclusion

"When you were born, you cried and the world rejoiced. Live your life so that when you die, the world cries and you rejoice."

- Cherokee Proverb

One of the many Cherokee myths details the journey to the Sun. Several young men took it upon themselves to traipse all the way across the world to witness the Sun rise and uncover what truly occurs. They met new tribes and people on the way, those that eat acorns or roots and those that burn widows when their husbands die. As they continued their journey, they ran into tribes that they had never heard of before. At last, when they reached the place where the Sun lived, they discovered how the Sky touched the ground. It acted as an open door, swinging open and close to let the Sun in and out. They watched the Sun emerge, a bright human-like being too hot to come close to, and one of the men tried to sneak in the open door before it shut. The large rock at the top of the Sky came crashing down on him and killed him. The others left, too afraid to tempt fate, and journeyed back home. However, their journey was so long that by the time they finally arrived home again, they were old, graying men.

The Cherokees' journey to the sunrise may never end. We've all heard the tale of Sisyphus, the tragic king of Ephyra. Hades punished him once he reached the afterlife by condemning him to an eternity of rolling a large boulder up a hill. However, the boulder rolls right back down as it nears the top, forcing Sisyphus to roll it up the hill once again. The story of the journey to the sunrise is not so different in essence—almost reaching the top, the conclusion, or the sunrise, only to retreat at the last minute.

Take a moment to consider the many journeys the Cherokee have been on. Collectively, they traveled across the eastern United States, steadily being forced out of their territory. Their story is the journey between an English allegiance and an American allegiance, of creating a syllabary, converting to Christianity, wearing new clothes, and adopting a judicial system and a written Constitution. Theirs is a journey of exile, tramping halfway across the United States barefoot on a months-long trek that resulted in death, illness, and suffering. They struggled to pick a side during the Civil War and were torn apart by tradition, cultural norms, and location.

It can hurt to peer back into the past with clean spectacles to uncover the truths about our ancestors, both those who were a part of what happened and those who were victims of it. The United States has granted its people many generosities, many rights, and many beloved things. But there's a duality to it, a truth that few are likely to admit.

So goes the journey into the past. We can never arrive at the final destination, but it's the learning along the way that changes the future. As the saying goes, "No river can return to its source, yet all rivers must have a beginning." In order to be better, stronger, healthier, and happier, we must take on the mantle of education and rediscover history in order to change our surroundings. To truly love something is to want it to be the best it can be.

Many students of the residential schools hid their traumas from the world. They tried not to share their stories, as they were ashamed, guilty, and traumatized by what had happened, but their behavior and actions betrayed the truth. Secretary Deb Haaland's movement to investigate all residential schools in the United States of America and uncover the true behind-the-scenes operations, as well as the mass graves too many of them contained, is a monumental shift in US history. By visiting the past, we are able to change the future. By learning about the atrocities committed at schools in the name of unification and assimilation, we can ensure that they will never occur again.

There is a Cherokee saying that goes like this: "Don't let yesterday use up too much of today." One should not allow the past to bog down today or tomorrow. However, using the past as a catalyst for change is not taking up too much of today or tomorrow. Instead, it's creating them and allowing the world to keep on turning.

As each day passes, citizens of the United States of America turn more and more to the Indigenous peoples of this land for their wisdom. Local farmers are turning to Native Americans for horticultural advice and knowledge. In order to grow our food, we must replenish the land first. Historians are marveling at early Native life, asking questions about how men and women managed to be equal in tribal societies in ways that have not been seen in the 21st century. The list goes on and on. To break the circle of hurt, trauma, and abuse, we must turn to the past and regard it with a fresh eye. It's always a good time to try and change tomorrow.

Black Elk, an Oglala Sioux Holy Man, once said,

> "You have noticed that everything an Indian does is in a circle, and that is because the power of the World always works in circles, and everything tries to be round... The Sky is round, and I have heard that the earth is round like a ball, and so are all the stars. The wind, in its greatest power, whirls. Birds make their nests in circles, for theirs is the same religion as ours... Even the seasons form a great circle in their changing, and always come back again to where they were. The life of a man is a circle from childhood to childhood, and so it is in everything where power moves."

Let us change the circle and make it a cycle of love, forgiveness, and healing.

Here's another book by Captivating History that you might like

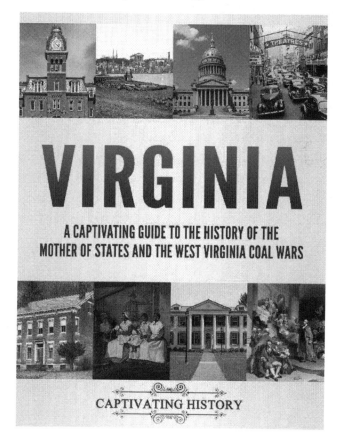

Free Bonus from Captivating History (Available for a Limited time)

Hi History Lovers!

Now you have a chance to join our exclusive history list so you can get your first history ebook for free as well as discounts and a potential to get more history books for free! Simply visit the link below to join.

Captivatinghistory.com/ebook

Also, make sure to follow us on Facebook, Twitter and Youtube by searching for Captivating History.

Endnotes

Anderson, David. "Paleoindian Period." New Georgia Encyclopedia, last modified
Jun 8, 2017.

Bailey, Matthew and Steven Nash. "Thomas R. R. Cobb." New Georgia Encyclopedia, last modified Mar 11, 2020.

Boney, F. ``Joseph E. Brown." New Georgia Encyclopedia, last modified Sep 30,
2020

Boulware, Tyler. "Cherokee Indians." New Georgia Encyclopedia, last modified Aug 24, 2020.

Bragg, William. "Reconstruction in Georgia." New Georgia Encyclopedia, last modified Sep 30, 2020.

Cashin, Edward. "Trustee Georgia, 1732-1752." New Georgia Encyclopedia, last modified Dec 10, 2019.

Callahan, Chrissy. "How's Jimmy Carter's Health? Grandson Shares Update after
Recent Illnesses, Injuries." TODAY.com, August 21, 2023.

Cobb, James and John Inscoe. "Georgia History." New Georgia Encyclopedia, last modified Sep 30, 2020.

Dendy, Larry. "University of Georgia." New Georgia Encyclopedia, last modified Jun 8, 2017.

Fink, Gary. "Jimmy Carter." New Georgia Encyclopedia, last modified Nov 3, 2020.

Getchell, Michelle. "The Civil Rights Act of 1964 and the Voting Rights Act of 1965 (Article)." Khan Academy. Accessed September 7, 2023.

Hatfield, Edward. "Eli Whitney in Georgia." New Georgia Encyclopedia, last modified Oct 31, 2018.

Hatfield, Edward. "Freedmen's Bureau." New Georgia Encyclopedia, last modified Sep 16, 2020.

Hatfield, Edward. "Segregation." New Georgia Encyclopedia, last modified Jul 20, 2020.

Hayes, John. "African American Baptists." New Georgia Encyclopedia, last modified Jul 26, 2017.

Hild, Matthew. "Farmers' Alliance." New Georgia Encyclopedia, last modified May 16, 2016.

Holzwarth, L. "The Reality of Debtor's Prisons in Britain and North America. History Collection, last modified Dec 8, 2022.

Huff, Christopher. "Wesleyan College." New Georgia Encyclopedia, last modified Apr 30, 2019.

Jackson, Edwin. "James Oglethorpe." New Georgia Encyclopedia, last modified Jul 21, 2020.

Justice, George. "Robert Toombs." New Georgia Encyclopedia, last modified Jun 8, 2017.

Lamplugh, George. "Yazoo Land Fraud." New Georgia Encyclopedia, last modified Jun 8, 2017.

Minchew, Kaye. "Franklin D. Roosevelt in Georgia." New Georgia Encyclopedia, last modified Aug 14, 2020.

Reid, R. "Howell Cobb." New Georgia Encyclopedia, last modified Sep 20, 2018.

Sassaman, Kenneth. "Stallings Island Site." New Georgia Encyclopedia, last modified Jun 8, 2017.

Saunt, Claudio. "Creek Indians." New Georgia Encyclopedia, last modified Aug 25, 2020.

Smith, Lillian. Killers of the dream: Negro Problem in Southern United States. Cresset Pr., 1950.

Storey, Steve. "Railroads." New Georgia Encyclopedia, last modified Sep 14, 2018.

Stout, Harry S. *The Divine Dramatist: George Whitefield and the Rise of Modern Evangelicalism (Library of Religious Biography)*. Print. September 9, 1991.

Tolnay, Stewart and E. Beck. "Lynching." New Georgia Encyclopedia, last modified Aug 12, 2020.

Tuck, Stephen. "Civil Rights Movement." New Georgia Encyclopedia, last modified Aug 24, 2020.

Wetherington, Mark. "Wiregrass Georgia." New Georgia Encyclopedia, last modified Sep 28, 2020.

Williams, David. "Gold Rush." New Georgia Encyclopedia, last modified Sep 12, 2018.

Williams, Mark. "Rock Mounds and Structures." New Georgia Encyclopedia, last modified Aug 21, 2013.

French, Laurence, and Jim Hornbuckle, editors. "Comments on the Cherokee Way of Life." *The Cherokee Perspective: Written by Eastern Cherokees*, Appalachian State University, 1981, pp. 44-114, https://doi.org/10.2307/j.ctt1xp3kws.8

O'Neil, Floyd A., et al. "The Indian New Deal: An Overview." *Indian Self Rule: First-Hand Accounts of Indian-White Relations from Roosevelt to Reagan*, edited by KENNETH R. PHILP, University Press of Colorado, 1986, pp. 30-46, https://www.jstor.org/stable/j.ctt46nr85.8

Nash, Philleo, et al. "The IRA Record and John Collier." *Indian Self Rule: First-Hand Accounts of Indian-White Relations from Roosevelt to Reagan*, edited by KENNETH R. PHILP, University Press of Colorado, 1986, pp. 101-09, https://www.jstor.org/stable/j.ctt46nr85.13

Irwin, Lee. "Cherokee Healing: Myth, Dreams, and Medicine." *American Indian Quarterly*, vol. 16, no. 2, University of Nebraska Press, 1992, pp. 237-57, https://www.jstor.org/stable/1185431

KRUPAT, ARNOLD. "Representing Cherokee Dispossession." *Studies in American Indian Literatures*, vol. 17, no. 1, University of Nebraska Press, 2005, pp. 16-41, http://www.jstor.org/stable/20737242

Benson, Sara M. "Territorial Politics: Mass Incarceration and the Punitive Legacies of the Indian Territory." *The Prison of Democracy: Race, Leavenworth, and the Culture of Law*, 1st ed., University of California Press, 2019, pp. 34-56, http://www.jstor.org/stable/j.ctvr7fd45.6

Lause, Mark A. "Solidarity: Coalescing a Mass Resistance." *Long Road to Harpers Ferry: The Rise of the First American Left*, Pluto Press, 2018, pp. 47-64, https://doi.org/10.2307/j.ctv69tg5b.6.

Davis, Ethan. "An Administrative Trail of Tears: Indian Removal." *The American Journal of Legal History*, vol. 50, no. 1, [Temple University, Oxford University Press], 2008, pp. 49-100, http://www.jstor.org/stable/25664483

Sturm, Circe. "Blood Politics, Racial Classification, and Cherokee National Identity: The Trials and Tribulations of the Cherokee Freedmen." *American Indian Quarterly*, vol. 22, no. 1/2, University of Nebraska Press, 1998, pp. 230-58, http://www.jstor.org/stable/1185118.

Smith, Andrea. "Boarding School Abuses, Human Rights, and Reparations." *Social Justice*, vol. 31, no. 4 (98), Social Justice/Global Options, 2004, pp. 89-102, http://www.jstor.org/stable/29768278

Dunbar-Ortiz, Roxanne. "THE INTERNATIONAL INDIGENOUS PEOPLES' MOVEMENT: A SITE OF ANTI-RACIST STRUGGLE AGAINST CAPITALISM." *Racism After Apartheid: Challenges for Marxism and Anti-Racism*, edited by Vishwas Satgar, Wits University Press, 2019, pp. 30-48, https://doi.org/10.18772/22019033061.6

Paul, Heike. "Pocahontas and the Myth of Transatlantic Love." *The Myths That Made America: An Introduction to American Studies*, Transcript Verlag, 2014, pp. 89-136, http://www.jstor.org/stable/j.ctv1wxsdq.6

French, Laurence, and Jim Hornbuckle, editors. "From The Cherokee One Feather, The Official Tribal Newspaper." *The Cherokee Perspective: Written by Eastern Cherokees*, Appalachian State University, 1981, pp. 206-40, https://doi.org/10.2307/j.ctt1xp3kws.13

Brown, Kent R. "Fact and Fiction: 'The Trail of Tears.'" *Journal of American Indian Education*, vol. 16, no. 2, University of Minnesota Press, 1977, pp. 1-6, http://www.jstor.org/stable/24397088

MILLS, MELINDA B. "Herbal Medicine Along the Trail of Tears." *Science Scope*, vol. 17, no. 6, Temporary Publisher, 1994, pp. 36-40, http://www.jstor.org/stable/43176915

Finkelstein, Norman. "History's Verdict: The Cherokee Case." *Journal of Palestine Studies*, vol. 24, no. 4, [University of California Press, Institute for Palestine Studies], 1995, pp. 32-45, https://doi.org/10.2307/2537756

Michelene E. Pesantubbee. "Nancy Ward: American Patriot or Cherokee Nationalist?" *American Indian Quarterly*, vol. 38, no. 2, University of Nebraska Press, 2014, pp. 177-206, https://doi.org/10.5250/amerindiquar.38.2.0177

Savage, Mark. "Native Americans and the Constitution: The Original Understanding." *American Indian Law Review*, vol. 16, no. 1, University of Oklahoma College of Law, 1991, pp. 57-118, https://doi.org/10.2307/20068692

Smith, Andrea, and J. Khaulani Kauanui. "Native Feminisms Engage American Studies." *American Quarterly*, vol. 60, no. 2, Johns Hopkins University Press, 2008, pp. 241-49, http://www.jstor.org/stable/40068531

Thornton, Russell. "Nineteenth-Century Cherokee History." *American Sociological Review*, vol. 50, no. 1, [American Sociological Association, Sage Publications, Inc.], 1985, pp. 124-27, https://doi.org/10.2307/2095346

Denson, Andrew. "Remembering Cherokee Removal in Civil Rights-Era Georgia." *Southern Cultures*, vol. 14, no. 4, University of North Carolina Press, 2008, pp. 85-101, http://www.jstor.org/stable/26391780

KRUPAT, ARNOLD. "Representing Cherokee Dispossession." *Studies in American Indian Literatures*, vol. 17, no. 1, University of Nebraska Press, 2005, pp. 16-41, http://www.jstor.org/stable/20737242

Blackburn, Marion. "Return to the Trail of Tears." *Archaeology*, vol. 65, no. 2, Archaeological Institute of America, 2012, pp. 53-64, http://www.jstor.org/stable/41781370

Bryant, James. "State Secret: North Carolina and the Cherokee Trail of Tears." *Journal of American Indian Education*, vol. 47, no. 2, University of Minnesota Press, 2008, pp. 3-21, http://www.jstor.org/stable/24398556

Finger, John R. "Termination and the Eastern Band of Cherokees." *American Indian Quarterly*, vol. 15, no. 2, University of Nebraska Press, 1991, pp. 153-70, https://doi.org/10.2307/1185121

Malone, Henry T. "The Cherokee Phoenix: Supreme Expression of Cherokee Nationalism." *The Georgia Historical Quarterly*, vol. 34, no. 3, Georgia Historical Society, 1950, pp. 163-88, http://www.jstor.org/stable/40577233

Satz, Ronald N. "The Cherokee Trail of Tears: A Sesquicentennial Perspective." *The Georgia Historical Quarterly*, vol. 73, no. 3, Georgia Historical Society, 1989, pp. 431-66, http://www.jstor.org/stable/40582012

Vestal, Stanley. "THE INDIANS OF OKLAHOMA." *Southwest Review*, vol. 14, no. 2, Southern Methodist University, 1928, pp. 138-52, http://www.jstor.org/stable/43465898

Jones, William S. "Bill." "The Legacy of the Trail of Tears in Van Buren County." *Tennessee Historical Quarterly*, vol. 63, no. 1, Tennessee Historical Society, 2004, pp. 48-52, http://www.jstor.org/stable/42627823

Pipestem, F. Browning, and G. William Rice. "The Mythology of the Oklahoma Indians: A Survey of the Legal Status of Indian Tribes in Oklahoma." *American Indian Law Review*, vol. 6, no. 2, University of Oklahoma College of Law, 1978, pp. 259-328, https://doi.org/10.2307/20068073

Coleman, Michael C. "The Responses of American Indian Children and Irish Children to the School, 1850s-1920s: A Comparative Study in Cross-Cultural Education." *American Indian Quarterly*, vol. 23, no. 3/4, University of Nebraska

Press, 1999, pp. 83-112, https://doi.org/10.2307/1185830

Wahrhaftig, Albert L. "The Tribal Cherokee Population of Eastern Oklahoma." *Current Anthropology*, vol. 9, no. 5, [University of Chicago Press, Wenner-Gren Foundation for Anthropological Research], 1968, pp. 510-18, http://www.jstor.org/stable/2740496

TREGLIA, GABRIELLA. "Using Citizenship to Retain Identity: The Native American Dance Bans of the Later Assimilation Era, 1900-1933." *Journal of American Studies*, vol. 47, no. 3, [Cambridge University Press, British Association for American Studies], 2013, pp. 777-800, http://www.jstor.org/stable/24485840

https://www.cherokeephoenix.org/news/1785-treaty-of-hopewell/article_321e6d88-2afd-5152-b0ea-d8238641ebaf.html
https://www.cherokeephoenix.org/ (Cherokee Phoenix, accessed Nov. 10, 2021)

https://www.narf.org/nill/documents/merriam/d_meriam_chapter1_summary_of_findings.pdf (Meriam Report Chapter 1, accessed Nov 14, 2021)

https://www.cherokee.org/about-the-nation/history/ (About the Nation, accessed November 6, 2021)

Made in the USA
Middletown, DE
01 March 2025